BWB Texts

Short books on big subjects
from great New Zealand writers

Kārearea

Māmari Stephens

Contents

Introduction 7

The Only Māori in the Room 9

Casual Racism and the Phone Message of Doom 14

I Never Saw Any Narrative of Māori Life Until I Was an Adult 18

Reading the Signs on a Journey into Māori Law 22

The Crown Isn't Just Pākehā – It Is Also Māori 35

What Some Bloody Awful Cartoons Can Tell Us About Ourselves 42

What About a Welfare System That Doesn't Judge Need? 49

Bad Laws Sometimes Deserve To Be Broken 56

Te Puea Marae, Tūhoe and the State of (Māori) Welfare 63

The Long Shadow Over Our Marae 73

Why Is God and Sexuality so Bloody Difficult? 85

In the Waiting Place 95

A Good Death 99

The Empathy Gap and Me 109

Teaching and Learning 119

Mana Wahine, the Legal System and the Search for Better Stories 125

Note on the Text 130

Notes 132

Acknowledgements 141

About the Author 142

About BWB Texts 143

Introduction

A kārearea is a beautiful creature. The picture in my mind's eye of a kārearea circling and watching the landscape below occurred to me when I was trying to think of a name and an image for my (then anonymous) blog. Somewhat ironically the main reason I started a blog was to be able to become practised at expressing my opinions and letting them go out in the world, without fearing the consequences of others ever seeing them. The kārearea's flight above has a comforting distance from the ground, after all. Maybe that could be me too. Of course it couldn't be, as I learned. It is not always necessary or even right to bring personal reflections into our own writing, but these pieces show how my writing often needs the people and experiences I come from, if my words are to make any sense at all. These columns are written from 2016–2020, and I miss them, really.

And the words make no sense at all without the people who love me, especially my darling Maynard, and our tamariki, Te Rangihuia, Havelund & Jessica-Lee. Ka nui te aroha, he aroha mutungakore, ki te Runga Rawa, ki a rātou hoki.

Tēnā koe.

The Only Māori in the Room

AUGUST 2016

I had one of those 'only Māori in the room' moments recently. I have a lot of those. These moments don't offend me. I work in mainstream tertiary education, I'm Māori and I profess to know something about things Māori. So what did I expect? Despite all that, these moments can be awkward. I was in a meeting about a research funding proposal with very clued-up academics from various faculties. The heads swivel in my direction as I'm asked my opinion on what I think the best direction for Māori would be, in regard to X or Y of the proposal.

There is a pause. Expectations hang heavy in the air. The words I say are to be weighed and perhaps given a weight disproportionate to their value. Or perhaps the reverse.

Sometimes, in moments like these, I can feel my cheeks flame. Sometimes, blind panic threatens to set in. On this occasion, however, I just snorted, laughed and said: 'Well, I don't know!' I may even have thrown my hands in the air.

That's usually how it is. I really don't know what Māori need, what Māori want, what direction would be best for Māori – how best to cater to, provide for, uphold and respect all things Māori. I have no portal into the Māori hive-mind. I take educated guesses in context. That's all I can ever do.

Of course, a lot of things had to happen for me to have been the only Māori in that room. The absence of other senior Māori academics weighs more on me than does the cumulative weight of Pākehā expectation. There has been recent research done on the experience of senior Māori and Pasifika academics, which gives us some insight into why this is.[1] Suffice to say, my experiences are hardly isolated, as a member of the 6 per cent of the academic workforce who identify as Māori.

Actually, my ruminations headed in a different, but related, direction. Because I'm not just assumed to be an ethnic representative of a people or peoples at moments like this. I'm expected to be a proponent of, and knowledgeable in, Māori culture to some degree.

Ah, culture. You marvellous double-edged sword, you.

After my meeting, I came home to a Facebook post that underscored the deep ambivalence I have towards our dominant notions of Māori culture. It was from an article outlining recent efforts being made to get young Māori into information technology:

> Computer graphics company Animation Research's founder Ian Taylor (Ngāti Kahungunu, Ngāpuhi) said the lack of Māori engagement in ICT was disappointing, as in his experience when Māori got their hands on technology they adapted very quickly.
>
> 'I believe that Steve Jobs, he didn't realise it – but he designed the iPad for young Māori. It wasn't in our DNA to use paper and pen, never has been. We use

our hands, we carve, we tell stories. We're great storytellers and technology has allowed us to engage in that way.'[2]

Reading this reminded me of another such moment in 2014 and another public statement from the prominent Māori educator Terehia Channings, of the recently closed Turakina Māori Girls' College. Speaking on the benefits of kapa haka for kids, she said (and I'm paraphrasing here): 'Well, Māori are practical people. We have problems with maths and science, we learn best with our hands.'

In both cases – and you don't have to search too far to find other such presumptions bubbling up among friends and whānau – an ossified understanding of Māori culture is held up and venerated. Māori people are practical. We make things and do things. We tell stories, we perform stories, but we don't write them down for others to read. And we probably don't read them either.

Forgive me if I take a moment to bash my over-educated head against a rather inviting red-brick wall.

Okay, I'm back.

I remember interviewing the Ngāti Porou and Ngāti Kahungunu actor and all-round extraordinary bloke Wi Kuki Kaa in 1992. He mused that people had often said to him that Māori were 'naturals' at acting, rugby and kapa haka. 'Nah,' he reckoned. In his view, if he had been raised in another family and in another culture, he would have been good at the things in those cultures. Māori weren't 'natural' at kapa haka. They were taught to be that way. There may be a genetic inheritance at work, but that can always be retooled in other cultures.

Culture is a human creation – that is all. It is the product of generations of people doing, saying, writing, thinking, eating, acting, singing, playing and being together. Rinse and repeat. There is no magic formula. There is no high-water mark of culture. There's no line we cross exactly when we know a cultural practice or a whole culture has died or forever changed. We just forget. And then we forget that we ever knew.

But culture, despite its blurred edges, performs an important function. Adherence to or membership of a culture (over and above mere ethnicity) grants us entry into something transcendent, beyond ourselves as individuals. Membership of a minority culture in particular gives us access not only to that culture and to a meaningful cultural life, but the rights of protection that accrue to that culture in international and domestic law. If there is no collation of practices, characteristics and products that can be identified as being of a given culture, then it cannot be protected.

On the one hand, we might tend to view culture as a mysterious unifying quality that marks out one set of human beings from another set of human beings. On the other hand, culture is a constraint. Once the hallmarks of a given culture are identified, reinforced and repeated, it becomes really difficult to challenge. Innovation and change pose huge risks to those who identify particularly with an Indigenous or minority culture.

So, the very moment we call on culture to help us advance a position, identify solutions to political problems, create unity and affirm kinship, it bites us on the backside and orders us back into the box of our own bloody making. There is no phrase that fills me with more dread than '*Māori are . . .*' And yet sometimes I use it. Because how else do we target and speak to Māori without identifying who we think Māori are? How do we employ Māori knowledge or seek it, without being open to seeing such knowledge is peculiarly Māori in the first place? How do we challenge Māori culture without first acknowledging that it exists?

I guess the answer is in common sense and moderation. We should reject essentialism – the idea that as Māori we're defined by an unchanging set of characteristics and behaviours – and the constraints it places on our evolution as a people. We should reject the position that sees no culture: that way lies cultural domination and oppression all over again.

And as for the Māori in the room? She'd better be a good tightrope walker, is all.

Casual Racism and the Phone Message of Doom

MAY 2017

I remember how much like a punch in the gut it felt to hear, at the age of sixteen, how my then-boyfriend's mother had said to him, 'Well, dear. It is not as if we will ever let you marry a Māori.' He reported this to me with a shake of his head and a laugh, until he caught sight of my reaction. I stared at him with my mouth open, my eyes welling with tears. I had been staying at his house with him and his parents in Wellington, and it was shortly before I was due to leave. She had said this awful thing even as I was staying under their roof. To be honest there was a little bit of context to that remark: he and I had been caught the previous evening in a little bit of a compromising position (cuddling on the same bed fully clothed, with door closed, in 1986, if you MUST know), and he had been trying to mollify her annoyance. So that was her ultimate riposte; I wasn't marriageable material anyway, so what did it matter what he did?

Once he saw my reaction my boyfriend realised, I think, how far over the line this comment was, and how painful it had been for me to hear. Actually, funny postscript... when I did leave, he and I went to the airport, and as we waited in the terminal, there was an announcement over the speakers that there was a phone call for me at the Air New Zealand desk. At the other end of the phone was his mother, apologising to me, and saying how she really didn't mean what she said, and what a wonderful person I was. And while I never married her son, in the years that followed, when I would visit, she always treated me with the greatest respect, and with real (so I felt) affection. I never held any long-term resentment over the comment; I just filed it away, I guess, under 'moments that make us figure out who we are, and who we are not'.

I was reminded of that moment this year when I read about the marae employee Blake Ihimaera receiving an unwelcome phone message, when the employee of the car company she was hiring from inadvertently failed to terminate the call, and he and his colleague had a moan about Māori people; they needed to be sent to their own island, and why the hell did they want their own prison anyway.[1] Blake described the moment she heard the message as being one where the bubble she had been living in burst. She had lived up until that time in a pro-Māori world, and this moment had shattered that bubble, maybe forever. I absolutely got that, that's how I felt. I knew, at my tender age then, that there was racism, and I knew Māori had had a bad deal (didn't quite know the details back then), but this was the first time I had really felt belittled by Pākehā directly for simply being who I was.

What I have learned in the intervening thirty years is that this kind of casual bigotry is endemic, but that it is only rarely a means to its own end. When my boyfriend's mother said what she said, of course it was racist. But it was also designed to hurt him because of the rule that we had broken. I was the means to her end of belittling him and his choices, more than anything else. We say the most awful things to the people we love the most. When I listened to the conversation between the car company employees, I heard that kind of racist 'locker room talk' between people who quite possibly don't know each other all that well, and are looking for ways to connect. And Blake, like me, was the means to that ignominious end.

So in that sense it's a mistake to call this racism casual at all; there was nothing casual about it in either event. The first example was one of deliberate punishment for transgression, and the second was a deliberate social strategy (or so it seemed to me). The awful thing in that second example is really how easily Māori people, or any people for that matter, are sacrificed to that long social process of building useful relationships. The things I have heard over my life about Chinese, Samoans, Iraqis, Somalians, Australian Aboriginals, when the speaker thinks he or she needs a bit of social lubrication to get by, are pretty depressingly awful. Many such bigoted comments have been made by Māori and Pasifika, unsurprisingly. And here's the thing: they almost always work. The raucous 'FAARK that's funny!' laughter, the raised eyebrows, the nod, the half shrug, the quiet 'yeah, well ...'. I have never seen anyone walk out of that kind of personal conversation, and that includes me, although I'm a lot better now at calling that kind of talk bollocks when I hear it than I was in my twenties or thirties. I have enough social capital that I can afford to lose some of it, you see.

It's easy enough to say, 'Well, just call it out. Call all that racist behaviour out, and if you put up with it you are as bad as they are. Boycott that car company for being racist bastards.' Yep, good call, consequences change behaviour, right?

Now let's look at our own lives and see how honest we *really* are in calling bigotry out when we see it. Or are we actually quite fond of it? Is this a dirty little secret tool that we actually do keep in our kete of social interactions? Maybe lots of us don't. I hope so. But my theory is we will sometimes put up with or promulgate outrageously untrue statements about large swathes of people we gleefully put to the sword, just for a moment of fellow feeling. Or perhaps we do it to make a point, or to punish someone, or whatever our immediate social need is at the time. And social media provides us with the massive echo chamber of bigotry to play around in. This comment on Facebook summed up the problem nicely:

> they should be sacked from their job not good enough that this is 2017 and we are still experiencing these racists remarks in our own country Damn white trash is all i can say

Doing it for the likes, right?

Ah, basic social anthropology I guess, in-group/out-group, nothing new to see here. But if we are to preside over the gradual death of 'casual' racism in our society we can't shame it into extinction if we don't also eradicate our own love of casual bigotry.

So. Sport and weather it is, then …

I Never Saw Any Narrative of Māori Life Until I Was an Adult

MARCH 2018

One evening, a few months ago, I found myself sitting on the couch opposite my fifteen-year-old son. We were both filling out a Harvard University online test, gauging our unconscious biases.[1] These tests, which make you hit specific keys in response to images of faces and words, are fun, and maybe not very accurate. At any rate, it turned out that I had a moderate unconscious bias *against* African-Americans and women. Oh, bloody marvellous. All my carefully nurtured social liberalism and bleeding-heart centre-leftism (with dashes of deep orthodox conservatism, truth be told) was rent asunder and I was left with the fact that, underneath it all, I remain a bundle of automatic reactions I can't control. As are we all, I guess.

My son though, showed a moderate unconscious bias *towards* African-Americans. He couldn't be bothered with the gender test and loped off to play Fortnite with his teen male mates, but still, he gives me hope. A hope that something in his growth and development, and in the images and people that he sees around him in his teen world, has gifted him better soil in which to nurture a more open view of people that look different from him.

Perhaps my (almost) relentlessly Pākehā-centric upbringing in 1970s Christchurch gifted me a different kind of soil. One that grew me into a person who has had to learn to not be afraid of difference. Hell, let's not beat around the bush – of course it did. It took years of very conscious effort for me not to be afraid to walk into a room full of people darker than I was. Despite my strong matriarchal upbringing and all-girls state education, it took years, too, to realise that male leadership and breezy male authority in all matters are not written in the stars. I still have to fight to over-compensate, even today, the day I turn forty-eight, for my own simple sexism and racism.

I think background is one thing, but also what really matters are the stories we tell ourselves, and the stories we hear or read. When I think back on the stories I immersed myself in as a lonely bookish kid, they were the staples of what I imagine a 1960s English childhood would be: *The Famous Five, The Secret Seven, Billy Bunter, The Hardy Boys*, Bullfinch's Greek myths, *Narnia*, and the occasional A.W. Reed story. My imaginary friends all had English accents and said 'My hat!' a lot. We watched a lot of Queen's Christmas Messages when I was growing up.

My movie memories are largely of the black and white and sometimes colour ones I'd watch with my mother on Sunday afternoons while she did hours and hours of ironing. I just don't remember, in the main, any stories with brown or black faces, unless they were the occasional Louis Armstrong or Sidney Poitier moment.

I don't remember female book heroes either (except for George in *The Famous Five* and Lucy in *Narnia*). I lived in a Pākehā visual bubble, with occasional Māori guest appearances from Prince Tui Teka and Billy T. James. There was simply no narrative of Māori life that I ever saw until I was an adult, and my own family story was too remote to create images in my head.

Things are different for my boy and I think his assumptions are different. He knows, very early in his life, where he comes from, and that he is Māori, which is just how it is. The predominant visual story surrounding him is still a Pākehā one, but *Boy* and *Dark Horse* are (boy-centric) stories that he will watch again and again, even as he pretends to do his reo Māori homework for school. Neither film reflects his own life really, but to him, they are just normal stories, just part of the Great Story of Everything. Perhaps his openness to diversity won't last. Who knows. Part of my job is to make sure he continues to see the world outside the bubble we have no doubt created for him.

So ever since he heard about this year's Māoriland Film Festival up in Ngāti Raukawa ki te Tonga country in Ōtaki (from 21 to 25 March 2018), he's been keen to go. Actually, he's not that interested in going to the movies of this festival – which, in its fifth anniversary year, is the 'most significant indigenous film festival of the southern hemisphere', according to the blurb.[2] To him, stories made by and about Māori or by and about other Indigenous peoples perhaps don't sound all that different from anything else, really. I think he wants to go because he's just never been to a film festival before, his uncle and aunty run it, and his Aunty Hinemoa will be down from Auckland. That'll do. What more do you need?

So, after work today (Friday, as I write) we'll drive in. There's a doco on late this afternoon, *Defending the Fire*, that promises to be a layered look at what we mean when we speak of a 'native warrior'. Maybe we'll sneak in to catch some of the Ookie-Spookies short films, perhaps the one about the Stállu a Sámi monster who is an outcast in society (*Slincraze Stállu*). Or the one about a young Aboriginal tracker hunting down criminals on the Australian Western frontier *(Blight)*.

Actually, we'll probably dine out on *Rumble: The Indians Who Rocked the World*, a feature documentary about the role of Native Americans in popular music history. The funny thing is that this movie will no doubt be revelatory to me, but not for my seriously musical son. My guess is, he'll be utterly unsurprised that there has been such an extraordinary Native contribution to popular music. He'll just enjoy the tunes, and effortlessly add this information to what he already knows is normal. We probably won't be there for the closing day on Sunday, but the programme, with a hundred movies in total, is full and rich right up until Sunday night.

Knowing my luck and his personality, my son will probably declare himself absolutely bored at some point and go find somewhere to hang out on his phone, while I'll continue to bask in images and sounds different from the ones I grew up with.

Normal transmission after all, then.

Reading the Signs on a Journey into Māori Law

FEBRUARY 2020

I'd like to say my journey into law and mātauranga Māori started with a great urge to fight for Māori people, to do right, to remedy injustices. But that is not how it started at all. It started, in a way, with a whack on the leg. My leg, that is.

Shift. Flicker. Focus.

In my mind's eye I was about ten or twelve, although, to be fair, every major memory of my childhood seems to stem from when I was about ten or twelve. In some ways I was a bit of a scared kid: scared of death, scared of the prospect of nuclear war and, in my heart of hearts, I was also scared of other Māori people. Other than my occasional timid forays into 'Māori Club' and a trip to Ahipara under the wing of my elder brother, I had no idea how to speak or understand te reo Māori. I had no clear idea that there was such a thing as tikanga Māori.

Until, that is, the day I sat on a little table in our lounge at home in Christchurch. I was wearing shorts. My brother walked in, saw me and, in a few quick strides, crossed the room and slapped my bare leg. Hard. I still remember the sound, and the shock, followed by confusion and shame.

'Never sit on tables,' he snapped.

I have never sat on a table since. At that point though, I had no idea *why* I couldn't. I had learned that I had crossed a line somehow, but I couldn't see the nature of the line, nor what lay on either side of it. I had learned I was subject to a law, but not why. My brother never slapped me again, but the lesson remained.

Shift. Flicker. Focus again.

It's 2013. We were about to go on to Korou Kore Marae in Ahipara for a wānanga: me and some other people I didn't know. I grabbed a cheap wrap-around skirt from the car boot. I knew enough about tikanga to offer a basic karanga; no one else seemed keen. Just as well, because my Aunty Mere was on the other side. She called, I called. We crossed the marae ātea.

I was relatively confident as we moved into the wharenui, I put myself in the back row on the visitors' side. I saw, but didn't truly see, that some of the others had gone up to stand in front of the pictures of tūpuna on the far wall of the wharenui for a moment or two before heading to the chairs. I paid no heed. I had done my job.

It was only much later that day when my Aunty Mere casually, yet very pointedly, let me know that it actually had been my job to lead the group up to the pictures, to allow due respect to be paid to those who had passed on before the whaikōrero could begin: 'It's what we do up here.' She sighed, 'You must have forgotten.'

No. I had not forgotten. I had never known. I knew something about karanga, but not enough. Up to this point, like many urban-based wāhine Māori, I had 'learned' karanga in an ad hoc way, without grasping much by way of nuance or learning how to read what was going on around me. This time when I learned of my transgression, there was no shock, just a dawning realisation, a sick feeling, heat in my face, and there it was again: shame.

Three decades or more on, and I understood a little better exactly where I had crossed the line. In the months and years afterwards I was able to pause, listen, learn and develop the way in which I did karanga. Aunty Mere has passed on now, but her gentle but utter deconstruction of what I thought I knew has always stayed with me.

Shift. Flicker. Focus again.

We all woke up to a crisp Ahipara morning and the rhythm of the distant early-morning surf. The tide was out, but there was to be no beach walk this holiday morning along Te Oneroa-a-Tōhē. My Australian-raised nephew Caleb had discovered the beginning of the Herekino walking track on the Awaroa–Kaitāia road. We were off – Caleb, his dad, Mark, our cousin Medadane and me – to try out the track.

We pulled up just after 7 a.m. and saw two signs at the track entrance. One was defaced, but we could still see the Department of Conservation logo and instructions for walkers to keep the forest safe from the disease of kauri dieback: SAVE OUR KAURI FORESTS! DON'T TAKE IN NON-PERMIT ANIMALS! SCRUB SOIL OFF SHOES! Or words to that effect.

Caleb and Mark disappeared beyond the darkness of the track entrance that was wreathed with green fronds. Yet Medadane and I stood still, looking not at the neglected DOC sign, but to the right of it, at a hand-lettered sign on fence boards in two sections, with the red letters maybe fifteen centimetres high: RAHUI I ROTO TE NGAHERE. Caleb hadn't really noticed either sign. Through no fault of his own, he could not have read the red one even if he had noticed it, and could not have known it said something like, 'prohibited in the forest'.

A rāhui had been imposed by local Māori from our hapū and iwi, our whanaunga. Medadane and I understood that the forest track had been made tapu, ritually restricted. But questions still flashed before me. When had the sign gone up? What was it for, exactly? Could the rāhui have expired? Who says when rāhui expire anyway? There was no signal on my phone, so we had no way to check. Ah well, no matter, the result was just the same. Medadane and I looked at each other, and then we shouted for the men to come back. We both understood we were forbidden from entering and that was that.

My mind scrolled quickly to the faces of a couple of senior women in our hapū who would be pretty cross if we simply blundered our way past the sign and into the inviting coolness of the track beyond. Heck, our photo might even end up on our Wainui Marae Facebook page or the Ahipara Takiwā page for all the hapū to see. Nup, the home people, the hau kāinga, call the shots here, not me, city-born Hone-come-lately that I have always been. 'Beach walk instead, whānau?' Medadane called. No rāhui there at the moment. Back to the car. No shame at all, this time.

These three minor moments show a haphazard development (of sorts) in my understanding of the existence of mātauranga Māori: in particular the way in which tikanga Māori comprises law. From vignette to vignette, like in scenes from an old Viewfinder, I am a slightly different person in each one.

In the first, I cannot see any sign of law that I ought to be observing, and only learn it exists through (transitory) pain and fear. In the second, I see it, and the duty I have to uphold, but I am ham-fisted and ignorant and I fail, at least in part, to discharge that duty. In the third, I see the sign, I read the sign correctly, I act on my reading of the sign, and so I reinforce our tribal collective's position with my obedience to the relevant tikanga.

In all three episodes I am with whānau, other family members, to whom I am somehow responsible. Whakamā, or shame, attends me in the first two, but I avoid her outstretched claws at the last.

The law of any people shows us (among other things) the lines that we ought not cross, and it also enables us to identify the line-crossers. Law reassures us of our own centrality and normality. All peoples are legal peoples, and all peoples to some degree consider themselves to be 'us' — bound by law of some nature, yet at the same time seeing those who are not so bound as 'them': not bound, not normal.

My journey into law and mātauranga is one more defined by absence, understanding of loss, whakamā, accident and a sense of coming in from the cold, than by any programmatic acquisition of expertise. In fact, up until my early twenties, Māori people and language had never really been normal at all to me. Māori concepts and ideas were not normal either, except in the most abstract and safe way. I had never really understood my own position as a child of the urban migrations; as a child emerging from earlier generations of my hapū, bearing its history and not even knowing it.

That position began to change as a result of learning basic te reo Māori for six months under the teaching and care of Niwa Short, Pererika Timutimu, Wilson Poha and others at kuratini (Wellington Polytechnic) in 1991. Until that point, I had had no visceral understanding of what or who had been lost by Māori, but the process of entering into te reo Māori and listening to others, as we had to shed our skins and learn about what we had lost, changed me forever and is still changing me now.

It also took me a long time to understand tikanga Māori as law by which I too could be bound. Like most people in this country, I grew up (in Christchurch with my Pākehā mum) presuming I was in a country with one complete legal system, to the extent I ever thought of such a thing existing at all. As far as I was concerned, we inherited this legal system, whatever that was, from the English, and that's why we have courts and Parliament and stuff like that, not that I paid attention to what they really did. I had a brother who joined the police very early in my life, so law enforcement and uniforms were benign to me; police were there to keep me safe, so I believed.

My unthinking acceptance of a single and all-encompassing legal system was reinforced in 1993 when, quite unexpectedly, I became a probation officer. I was an underemployed radio programme-maker in Wellington and in a burst of curiosity one day I walked into the Community Probation Service on Thorndon Quay, then in the old Tramways Building, wondering if they had any jobs. I had trained in radio broadcasting at polytech, I had been working in Māori broadcasting at Te Upoko o Te Ika Wellington Māori Radio station on Lambton Quay and I had little idea what a probation officer even was. Could I be one? I was twenty-three, needed a better income and had few clues.

Martin Roberts was the duty probation officer on that day, and answered my questions with patience and grace. A few weeks later he rang me and offered me a temporary job. I spent the next seven years jobbing as a probation officer, learning how to apply the Criminal Justice Act 1985, write pre-sentence reports, make sentence recommendations and supervise people on community-based sentences and on parole.

For the most part, I never questioned my role in this system I had become a tiny part of. I learned a great deal from experienced officers like Martin, Fiona Kale, Etai Morgan, Marian Kleist, Trevor Shoesmith, Audrey Moonlight, Murray Olsen and others. I learned about public service, integrated offender management systems and government policy. I learned about servicing the court. I learned how to pitch my sentencing recommendations to judges in such a way that they would be more likely to be accepted. I learned little about Māori experiences in the criminal justice system. Or more accurately, I paid little attention.

On the other hand, there I met my husband-to-be, Maynard Gilgen, a Department of Corrections psychologist at the time, and it was he more than anyone else who helped me see that just as language loss was a deliberate policy, the legal system we were working in had never been inevitable and was not immutable. It was, and remains, the institutional result of choices made, though not by Māori. Its disproportionate and calamitous impact upon Māori has never been an accident, but is central to its design and operation. His long-held anger and grief for Māori, for our people, worked further cracks into my unthinking acceptance of the status quo that had protected me from truth for so long.

It was from this time in the early- and mid-1990s, slowly, so very slowly, and helped by a lot of people wiser than me, that I began to understand the Māori world as more than a set of abstract ideas, surviving artefacts and compulsory ritual that I could simply learn and acquire like a series of badges.

A couple of years into my probation life, our colleague and mate Etai Morgan suggested to me one day that I'd make a good judge. After my initial snort of disbelief, this suggestion prompted me to at least think about studying law. Could it be harder than probation work?

I had little knowledge of lawyers. I don't think I had ever met one when growing up or before my time in Corrections, I knew nothing of what they did, other than what I saw on television shows like *Law and Order*. I had just started studying te reo Māori and classics at uni anyway, so the next year I added first-year law and surprised myself by loving it and getting good marks.

I have no recollection of Māori-specific learning in law that year, but I remember how few other Māori law students there were. Actually, noticing Māori absence was a hallmark of my university study. In studying Greek mythology and what it teaches us about ancient Greek society, I wrote essays about Māori mythology and what that teaches us about Māori society, old and modern. In my law study it was not surprising, then, that I began to wonder what Māori law was, where it could be learned and understood. In jurisprudence classes, I wrote about what the jurisprudential theorist H. L. A. Hart meant when he wrote about 'primitive law', and I wondered what he would have made of tikanga Māori.

With occasional exceptions, such as the Māori land law course, I was not learning anything specific about mātauranga Māori or Māori law in my law degree. Yet in 1997 contract law classes, Tony Angelo taught us the story of Ponga and Puhihuia and how that story could reflect Māori notions of contract. This was a revelation to me: that Māori *narratives* could reveal *law*; they could show the lines and what could happen when these were crossed or violated.

After saying goodbye to Corrections at some point, I graduated in law and in 2002 ended up working for Martin Dawson in the Māori legal team at Russell McVeagh ('Ngā Manu Tāiko') first as a summer clerk, then in a graduate position, and then as a solicitor. I learned that this Pākehā man believed with all his heart that Aotearoa had been Māori land and remained Māori land until Māori said otherwise. He had an abiding faith in the relevance of mātauranga Māori, and in Māori people, and in us, his small team, and in the ability of lawyers to help bring about change for the better.

When he died in 2003, taking a little bit of all our hearts with him, not long after I had had my first son, I wanted to do something that he would approve of, perhaps even be proud of. A couple of years later I had my chance; I became a lecturer at the Faculty of Law of Victoria University.

In the first year of holding that privileged position, I had a realisation while on maternity leave with my second child. The general legal system of New Zealand has at its disposal an enormous wealth of Māori-language law-related source texts dating back to the early nineteenth century, as Māori had sought from the earliest days of contact to understand and interact with Pākehā ways of doing things, including law both sacred and secular. Many of those Māori language texts still remain relatively unexplored, as yet, but in those texts resided a Māori legal language and terminology. By seeing the almost complete absence of mātauranga Māori in the study of New Zealand law, I realised that te reo Māori, despite all that colonisation had thrown at it, has always been an ordinary language of law and civic discourse. Te reo Māori, in fact, was an inevitable vehicle for mātauranga Māori. This language and its knowledge had always existed inside and outside of the monolithic legal system, and we needed to pay attention to it.

To cut a long story short, I was part of the Legal Māori Project based at the Law Faculty that collated a corpus of reo Māori sources, compiled and, along with my friend and colleague Dr Mary Boyce and many others, built a dictionary of legal Māori terms (*He Papakupu Reo Ture*, LexisNexis, 2013), and created a set of related online resources, including an online dictionary (the Legal Māori Resource Hub at www.legalmaori.net). I think Martin would have been proud of that.

My own inconsequential learning, stumbling and experiences of whakamā, along with those research experiences of looking for absences and seeing Māori legal language and concepts at work in pulling together the dictionary, has shown me the normality and ordinariness of tikanga Māori as laws by which I and other Māori can also choose to be bound as circumstances decree.

Any exploration of tikanga Māori should look to the wealth of oral and written Māori textual and linguistic evidence that is so far under-explored. Such evidence can illustrate ordinary modern and historical practices of Māori communities (such as hui, or decision-making gatherings, as the pre-eminent forum for the generation of Māori law) with all their variety and their changes over the course of centuries. These practices in turn reveal very specific concepts and values, of relevance to law. The knowledge of these practised values is transmitted over time from person to person, within and between Māori collectives such as whānau, hapū and iwi.

Such practised values will be at the heart of tikanga, although tikanga cannot just be reduced to a set of rules. Without relying on a centralised institution or set of institutions, tikanga itself is not only made up of the rules of behaviour, but also comprises the mode for determining when such rules ought to be used. Tikanga also enables the setting of standards for evaluating the proper use of such rules. In reality, there is no unified or consistent way in which tikanga appears to be viewed in Māori thinking and practice, but undoubtedly tikanga shows us what is valued within specific Māori collectives at any given time.

These practices, standards and values are discoverable but, as other Indigenous peoples around the world have found, there are serious gaps due to a fracturing of tikanga Māori that has occurred as a result of colonisation, war, urbanisation and modern Māori life. Notwithstanding this, we need good scholarship that generates sound mātauranga Māori and shows the operation of Māori law in all its fracturedness and sometimes wholeness. I have done little more than hint at what mātauranga Māori can add to our full understanding of law in Aotearoa New Zealand. I hope to do more in my current and future research and teaching.

There are small signs that the New Zealand legal system and New Zealand society as a whole is starting, slowly and reluctantly, to pay attention to mātauranga Māori, including Māori law, as a matter of relevance to all who inhabit this land. For years now, Sir Joseph Williams has been reading the signs and outlining the possibility of a third way of law, a 'Lex Aotearoa' that incorporates Māori law (or Kupe's law, as he terms it) and Cook's law. That third way is where we in the legal research world need all the help we can get, as we look for new lines and new boundaries, and consider anew what we are really bound by.

When a rāhui was imposed in December 2019 by Ngāti Awa after the eruption of Whakaari and the death of nineteen people, the ritual prohibition was observed by most, if not all: Māori and non-Māori alike.

In that moment of trauma, and maybe just for that moment, we had all learned to read the signs and see the line.

The Crown Isn't Just Pākehā – It Is Also Māori

OCTOBER 2017

Symbols come in many forms, tangible and the intangible. They tell us stories we may not even be aware of.

Here's one. I work in a beautiful building. It is a building that breathes and moves about me. Occasionally, as I walk down the halls or the stairway, I feel surrounded by a soft golden glow, created by the sensory fusion of kauri finishings, scroll-shaped corbels, the curved window bays, and sombre carpeting. Mostly, I just feel harried and inadequate, so I forget to marvel at this hand-wrought architectural icon.

'Icon' is the right word because these Old Government Buildings in Wellington operate as a transportive symbol. Walk through the doors and, whether or not you are aware of it, you are carried to an era of history that consolidated New Zealand as a colonial nation. Built in 1876, the year provincial governments were abolished and a central government established, *this* place was the seat of administrative power. This building tells a simple surface story of a young nation finding its way, but the deeper and truer story is of Pākehā power and claim surmounting the messy, contested and uncertain history of several peoples.[1]

So I walk the victors' halls. As a law lecturer, I now teach aspects of the legal system that upholds that deeper story, as those halls now comprise Victoria University's law school. You will see no koru, no tukutuku, no whakairo. There are Māori and Pasifika spaces tucked away, fragile and lovely, if you know where to look – retrofitted exceptions to this narrative of solidity and permanence.

Most of us who work and study in this place don't pay attention to this contest of stories. And fair enough too. We have our lives to get on with and futures to imagine. It's our building, we use it, we inhabit it for a brief time (or maybe for a long time) on our way to somewhere else.

Let's not overthink things, right?

In the 2017 pre-election maelstrom you might have missed a pretty insignificant story. I nearly did, bewitched as I was by Jacinda, Gareth and Marama et al. (not always in that order). It was a little item on the TV news (and in the Christchurch *Press*) in mid-September about people lining up to see inside the new $300 million justice and emergency services precinct, including the police watch-house and cells.[2]

> Thousands jumped at the chance, with the queue stretching down Lichfield St all morning and into the afternoon. …
>
> 'It's quite unreal really, definitely a different experience,' one said. 'The kids love it which is great.'
>
> They'll just be hoping this is the only visit they'll have to make to the police cells.[3]

Somehow this event pierced my election-induced fog. I paused, wondering if I'd heard it correctly. I waited for the punchline, or the ironic comment. There was none. This little, unimportant story symbolised something larger. Apparently, in my hometown, thousands of happy people queued for more than an hour to see the inside of a legal system, which they accepted was theirs but was not designed to punish *them*. To such people there is *right*, as well as *rightness* in the process and the outcome of law. Law is normal, formal, probably a bit absurd and creaky, but part of the natural order of things.

Five days later the almost exact opposite occurred, also at the symbolic level. In celebrating Māori Language Week, a police car decked out in te reo Māori decals made its debut in Papakura, Auckland. The response was, shall we say, mixed:

> 'Been to Ngā Whare Wātea today and the kids were all over it. It was fantastic, they had a great time,' says police officer Ivan Tarlton (Ngāpuhi).

However, not everyone is smiling.

> Khylee Quince: 'Waitangi Tribunal earlier this year, only five months ago, makes recommendations about the Crown breach of Treaty relationships and Treaty duties, particularly active protection in relation to Māori and the terrible disproportionate rates of Māori offending.[4] This is the first we see from the police in response to that, so particularly poorly thought-out strategy in my view.'

> Julia Whaipooti, of the youth-led rights organisation JustSpeak, is one who expressed concern: 'Putting a

> kupu Māori on a police car doesn't seem to form part of any strategy towards reducing the number of Māori we have entering and being processed in the system at disproportionate rates. It's like having a pōhiri to come into prison. Putting a Māori name on a police car doesn't do anything to address the issues.'[5]

Similar feelings had been expressed months earlier when the Department of Corrections launched a new haka to find new recruits, in part as 'a challenge for Māori to step up and accept the role of being a change agent working as a Corrections Officer'.[6] Others saw such symbolic developments as ineffective bandaids for the vast problem of Māori hyper-incarceration.[7]

The haka and the Māori design on the police car were symbolic of a powerful story, just as powerful as that represented by my workplace: Māori could only be subject to the legal system, never owners of it. Māori (most, not all) will never have unthinking ownership of Crown or government institutions. Most (not all) Pākehā New Zealanders, in comparison, assume exactly such ownership.

There's an example from my own work life that I have blogged about before, of the daily and undramatic reality that underpins such symbolism.[8] Every year I have a similar kind of student visit me, and we have a version of the following conversation:

> 'I'm having trouble with my lectures. I just don't get it.'
> 'Okay. What are you finding so hard?'
> 'I don't understand what the lecturer is saying. I write

down everything she says. I read it, again and again, I highlight the words, and I write it out again and I still don't get it.'

'Okay. Show me some of your notes. Right. Do you know what this is [pointing to "Cabinet Minister"]?'

'Not sure.'

'What about this [pointing to the word "statute"]?'

'Not sure about that either.'

'How about this [pointing to the word "Parliament"]?'

'I know where it is, I just don't know what it *does*.'

This student may have already struggled with the education system, but not necessarily. She may well be a B student in her other subjects, but the ideas behind words like 'statute', 'Parliament' and 'Cabinet Minister', for the moment at least, defeat her. She has never, in her life, come across them before in a way that enabled her to understand them. Perhaps she didn't come from a family where politics or voting, or even the news, were discussed, where Western 'law' was ever really thought of as something beyond 'what the police do'.

This student is Māori, but her lack of exposure to the most basic ideas of Western 'law' doesn't stem just from ethnicity, because I've also had these conversations with Pākehā, although *far* more rarely. She merely falls on the difficult side of social and educational history. Like many other Māori in tertiary study (including me and my brothers) she is the first of her family to study at uni, the first to study law. She has no template to follow and, for whatever reason, school didn't prepare her by introducing her to the ideas underpinning our institutional structures. Right now, she has absolutely no confidence that this will ever be her world or her tool. How can she? She can't even describe it yet. Our general system, our law in all its manifestations, is alien and abnormal. It's an animal to study behind safety glass. A poisonous exotic.

Strangely enough for those who do have that sense of ownership of our general legal system, Māori law has become the alien. The museum exhibit. The quaint but useless curiosity.

And yet there are signs that this kind of rigid dualism in thinking is outliving its usefulness.

There is a sentence in the reo section of the Wai 262 Flora and Fauna report that hit me one day in 2010, and I've repeated it many times to myself ever since.

> Fundamentally, there is a need for a mindset shift away from the pervasive assumption that the Crown is Pākehā, English-speaking, and distinct from Māori rather than representative of them. Increasingly, in the twenty-first century, the Crown is also Māori. If the nation is to move forward, this reality must be grasped.[9]

The Crown is also Māori. This extraordinary statement is at once surely true and surely incapable of being true. When exactly does reality collapse into one possibility or the other, I wonder? Acceptance of the notion that the Crown is also Māori requires reaching beyond the idea of simply negotiating better Māori space. Or better concessions for Māori. Or a Māori seat at the table. Such a notion requires the development of an unthinking assumption that the table is Māori to start with; that the Old Government Buildings are to be understood to be as much a Māori as a Pākehā construct.

A few weeks ago I was one of the moot court judges for the internal Māori moot at Te Herenga Waka Marae. It was a competition where Māori students put arguments before judges in a mock court setting. Of the six students, four mooted in Māori. Each of them was able to move fluidly between an unconscious ownership of the legal system and of tikanga Māori, and a blistering critique of the same systems. Just one small symbolic and up-ending moment of something better. There are other such moments waiting to coalesce.

In truth I doubt the Old Government Buildings can ever really be understood to be as much a Māori space as a Pākehā construct, even if we did add whakairo and other symbols of Māori ownership to it. I'm looking for the day when more Māori can walk through the doors with their culture intact, and are indeed transported: not to an era of colonial power made manifest, in which they are an exception to an unwritten rule, but simply to a place they own. Unthinkingly.

What Some Bloody Awful Cartoons Can Tell Us About Ourselves

MAY 2017

I don't get personally offended easily. I learned a while ago not to buy too much into the fever-dreams of keyboard warriors – and most of the people around me who do say outrageous things are not loathsome people, so I don't care to waste my energy in policing them. And I'm lucky, I think, to have avoided some of the more obvious slings and arrows of racist misfortune in my life.

Except, I haven't. Not really. I'm a child of the urban migrations and the lost Second World War generation. Before that, a descendant of colonial wars. And before that, of inter-tribal musket wars, and all the upheavals and trauma – political, demographic and spiritual – in between. I am who I am because of the collective Te Rarawa and Māori experience of intergenerational losses — including the loss of language, place and space, tribal connection, knowledge, and sheer entitlement. As an Anglican, I'm also heir to the good and the bad of church history, particularly in the North and Waikato. Of course, I am the sum of other things as well – my Irish and German forebears and their respective histories – but those things lie lightly on me.

Just because I have a pretty peaceable nature, it would be easy to mistake someone like me, on face value, for being 'balanced'. Not likely to fly off the handle. Someone who isn't too 'PC'. Probably so, but I carry the weight of Māori history, like any other 'descendant of a New Zealand Māori', to use that quaint phrase of legislative definition.

And for many of us from Māori families and communities, the historical losses don't tell the whole story, compounded as it is by the accumulation of many little and large unintentional slights, deliberate hurts and omissions over years of racism and bigotry that can be forgiven, but can't be wished or washed away. Or unfelt, or unseen, or unheard.

Yet we're expected in the eyes of many (not all, of course) simply to be 'good sports'. Come on, let the mispronunciation rest, let the accusation of theft pass, let the suspicious glance lie, live down to that low expectation, let the stereotype alone. Oh, grow a sense of humour and just let the past be. Don't be so easily offended. No matter how that past calcifies around us like an oddly inefficient shell: porous enough to let the hurt through, and unyielding enough to last through generations.

So, as 'good sports' we know the engineering students' bastard 'haka', performed annually for twenty-five years, ending in 1979, was just a generation-long harmless joke.[1] The deliberate and non-deliberate butchering of Māori names on our airwaves and in our classrooms is just something to be borne — don't make a fuss. Naked selfies on a sacred maunga are just awesome T & A photo ops. Artists, academics and government officials alike can, like magpies, pinch the shiny bits of the language out of dictionaries for their signs, their academic papers, their artworks, without ever being able to speak a complete sentence in the language, let alone know what it means. Yes, we will sit for your portrait, we will die on your canvas, your tote bag, your tea towel. We will be the noble savage of your dreams.

Hey, it's OKAY. You're welcome.

But a small thing is never just a small thing, right?

Of course, Māori can never claim a monopoly on the experience of racism and bigotry, and grievance is not a state of grace we should seek to hold on to. But just like the violent and heavy histories, the stories we tell and retell of small (and big) moments of everyday ignorance and racism are indigenous to Aotearoa as well: formed of this soil and of this air, and in this land of shifting light. And sometimes, just for the purpose of release, those stories must be told and retold with fresh anger each time, as Amie Berghan Paulet shows by sharing some of the words on the tip of her tongue:

> Racism is when you label my people 'dole bludgers'.
> Racism is when you tell my people to just 'get over it, the past is the past'.
> Racism is when you look at the 'statistics' and not the truth that is hiding behind the statistics.
> Racism is when discussing history you expect my people to walk towards you for healing instead of you walking towards us.
> Racism is when you take naked selfies on our sacred mountains and then label us as 'prudes' or pass over our

offence as if it's because we don't understand freedom to self-expression.[2]

It's true that Māori are asked to forgo much in order to preserve the sanctity of 'freedom to self-expression'. Up to the limit of the law, of course.

Right. So, what is the limit of the law? Al Nisbet can help us there.

Do you remember, from a few years back, his cartoon caricatures of waddling Māori bludgers with their smokes and their alcohol and the glint of greed in their beady, calculating eyes? The ones with the dull, bloated children with stunted futures and dubious parentage? Remember *those* cartoons?[3] Well, unsurprisingly, some of us got upset when they were published back in 2013, and Louisa Wall and South Auckland youth group Warriors of Change took *The Press* and *Marlborough Express* newspapers to court. Well, more specifically, to the Human Rights Review Tribunal.

When the decision came in, according to the Tribunal, the cartoons, offensive as they are, did not breach the Human Rights Act 1993.[4]

How does this happen?

First off, where does this right to freedom of expression come from anyway? This magic notion, that is as limitless as human thought and imagination, is set out in s14 of the New Zealand Bill of Rights Act. And let's be clear – the right is not absolute. It has limits, including limits imposed by law.

Including this bit of law: Section 61(1) of the Human Rights Act 1993. According to this, it is unlawful for any person to publish or distribute written matter that is threatening, abusive or insulting – and likely to excite hostility against or bring into contempt any group of persons on (in this case) the basis of race.

It's not hard to find those cartoons insulting towards Māori, and the Tribunal agreed. Those cartoons could indeed go straight to the top shelf of small and large things designed to add to the weight of everyday bigotry and racism. Straight to the pool room, even.

It's the last requirement that's the hardest: it's a causation test. Words – or images, as here – can't merely be hurtful and degrading or insulting. They actually have to be likely to cause other people to become hostile towards Māori on the basis of race.

To cut a long story short, the Tribunal said no. The cartoons didn't reach that threshold. Case closed. And regardless of what I'm about to say below, in the main, I agree with the result. Simply to live in this society we have to allow those around us to say horrible things we don't like, even if those things wound us. And they do. In turn, we have the same ability to insult, wound, and offend. My Facebook feed is replete with people (often brown ones) gleefully taking up the opportunity to rip into others. This is part of our jostling co-existence – and the cost to our own freedom to insult and offend and express whatever we want would be too great to close down the Al Nisbets of this world, even though his work adds to our burden of racist experiences.

But I did want to call your attention to something else in the Tribunal's judgment.

In evaluating whether Nisbet's cartoons were likely to

incite hatred, the Tribunal, as directed by the Supreme Court in an earlier case, had to turn to that marvellous legal fiction: the 'reasonable person'. You see, how do we know if insulting words are likely to excite others to be hostile towards Māori? Well, that depends on someone who has never existed – the reasonable person. A kind of paragon of circumspect behaviour who just happens to be lurking around at the time when these published images hit the public arena. This sensible and sober person would have some knowledge, so would know that the cartoons show Māori people, would have some idea of the stereotypes in play, and would know about local conditions and community. Would that reasonable person, aware of the context and circumstances surrounding the use of the words, view them as exposing Māori to hatred among other people?

But here's the thing. The 'reasonable person' is not allowed, in the context of the Human Rights Act 1993, to be Māori. Not in this case, and probably not ever. The focus is not on how greatly Māori were injured, but on how likely *non*-Māori were to become hostile as a result. As the Tribunal said:

> In the present case the cartoons were unquestionably about a subject of public interest; they were also provocative. That Māori and Pacifika were offended and insulted is not the point. Section 61 is directed not to the effect on them, but on the effect on non-Māori and non-Pacifika and the likelihood of their being excited to hostility against Māori and non-Pacifika or their holding Māori and Pacifika in contempt. In our view the cartoons

were insulting but fell well short of bringing Māori and Pacifika into contempt.[5]

See, I imagine a reasonable person who *can* be Māori, who can emerge out of the context within which Māori live, who can appreciate the weight of history and everyday bigotry on the hearts and minds of Māori people. I imagine a reasonable Māori person who can see that, and still value freedom of expression.

But the Tribunal couldn't really explain to me why it is that the reasonable person in this case and in our general legal system is never Māori.

Perhaps we carry too much weight, too much hurt, you see, to ever be trusted to be truly reasonable. Or truly normal and ordinary.

Just maybe the Māori reasonable person has no sense of humour.

What About a Welfare System That Doesn't Judge Need?

APRIL 2017

A couple of weeks ago, on a Lower Hutt street, a woman and her children decided to do something kind for someone else. They gave carefully chosen and prepared food to a homeless man. A few moments later, they drove past the same area again, only to see that this man had thrown the food all over the street. The woman posted about the dismay she and her children felt at this apparent rejection of their kindness. The story was picked up by the *New Zealand Herald* and garnered much feverish comment.[1]

The social media response was fascinating to me. It was somewhat split between those who believed the man in the story to have been ungrateful, or simply insufficiently poor. Others presumed him to have been sufficiently poor, sufficiently destitute, but probably afflicted with a mental health condition that might have explained his response.

Interestingly there was also a thread of comments from people who reckoned they knew him – that they were familiar with his behaviour and with what motivates him day-to-day. Some who claimed such knowledge saw him as an ingrate who was rorting the system:

> I have a shop that he sits outside on a regular basis. The owner of the dairy next door gave him food which he then threw all over the ground outside my shop. He knows exactly what he was doing as he comes in to my shop and wants to borrow our pens to write his signs. His actions are completely calculated. He does not eat food he only wants cash. He is completely ungrateful and very confronting.

Others with a degree of knowledge saw the same person differently:

> So I've had food thrown at me by the same guy after I brought it for him. It's fair to point out that since then I've learnt that he has severe mental health issues and is extremely picky about what he eats. I initially wanted to beat him up but after learning about him a bit I definitely wouldn't. Apparently he's a lovely guy.

It was interesting to me to see how knowledge about the man in the story became a kind of currency. The more we knew about him, perhaps the more we felt we could be justified in saying: 'Yes, he deserves compassion' or 'No, he doesn't deserve compassion'. Thus, we are entitled to judge if genuine need exists. Once we put ourselves in the position of judging the existence of need, we must inevitably find some people worthy and others unworthy of help. How do we know what your needs are if you don't show us good and sufficient evidence of it? The man in the story failed in this regard. Or succeeded – depending on your perspective, your values, your knowledge, your prejudices.

There is no point whatsoever in bemoaning these kinds of comments or beliefs. Quite literally, they are centuries old, and were brought to New Zealand with European (mainly were English) settlement. It started with the mainly (but not exclusively) Christian notion that we all have a duty to provide for the poor. Over time, that duty became so bureaucratised and formalised in charitable systems, and later social security systems, that the religious aspect has faded from memory, but the bureaucratic urge to judge deservingness has not. This belief that need must be shown before aid will be given is deeply ingrained in the history and bureaucratic culture of this country. Neoliberalism only enhances this tendency – it certainly did not create it.

And why blame others for this judginess anyway, when we all engage in this thought process? Think of our own experiences with those asking us for money, be they charity collectors, individuals on the street, or school fundraisers. In each case our internal decision-making processes spring from our own personal well of discretion, and are formed by our own internal values. Our private processes are pretty similar to millions of decisions being made all around the country by charity and government workers every year, springing from their own official or informal discretion. Rules and regulations abound, but at the heart of government welfare and charities are individuals making judgments: Help or not? Deserving or not? Right or wrong? Pay or not?

It is this drive to judge that justifies our intrusion into the lives of the people who we would support, if only they are 'genuine'. This drive to judge is also highly susceptible to our basest presumptions about the colour and culture of others. Māori and Pasifika are, by definition, poor and, in the minds of some, by definition, undeserving and morally and culturally suspect.

Our most sophisticated and yet intrusive manifestation of this drive is in our welfare system. It is primarily a needs-based system that eradicates differences between people. Assistance only depends on individuals showing sufficient need, and sufficient effort to first meet it themselves. Those responsible for delivering the aid are duty bound in law to investigate such claims of need.

While in criminal law there are buffers or protections put in place to protect the individual in that system from state intrusion - *except* where criminal liability is proved - the welfare state creates the *opposite* effect. In return for assistance, the state has the right, and increasingly so, to approve the actions, the household formations, the drug-taking behaviours, the social connections, the parental behaviours of beneficiaries. There is no buffer between the state and the person. All is justified in the pursuit of the demonstration of need.

There are a few treasured exceptions where individuals do not have to show they have reached the hallowed status of need. For example, in superannuation, need does not have to be shown. It is usually *presumed* once applicants reach the age of sixty-five. As an aside, it always puzzles me how superannuitants are vocal in insisting that superannuation is not a benefit, that it is somehow different in form and shape – that superannuation is an earned entitlement for taxes paid and lives well lived.[2] Well, maybe, but by law, superannuation is defined as a benefit. It is administered as part of the benefit system, it is governed by the same review and appeal system, and it forms part of the same item in the Crown Accounts. It is a walking and quacking benefit duck.

I am a great believer in the universality of Super, not least because for the majority of cases (not all), the state doesn't get to hide under the bed, poke through the medicines on the bedside cabinet, and count the toothbrushes in the bathroom. I also happen to believe that universality is necessary to address child poverty in New Zealand – that children and their parents ought not have to show need, that need should be presumed. Childhood, like old age, is a hazardous state. We ought to take collective responsibility for it, and, in the language of Jess Berentson-Shaw, water the whole garden, not just the bits we like better.[3]

But even adding a universal child benefit to our existing system doesn't change its fundamental nature. In a very real sense it doesn't matter who the government is, it doesn't matter how the labels on the benefits get changed around, the system remains, and the law around the use of discretion and entitlement stays largely the same. Of course, it matters in the immediate context because under National-led governments entitlements get squeezed, efficiency is valorised; and under Labour there is generally a lessening of a punitive approach and a loosening of work-testing requirements. But the primacy of need and the shape of the system (including the current

Social Security Legislation Rewrite Bill before the House) remains unchallenged.[4]

Changing the system requires a revolution in thought we are just not ready for yet. Or are we? I have written before about the possibility of Tūhoe creating their own welfare system, invoking a possible devolution of Crown liability for Tūhoe welfare.[5] Gareth Morgan and The Opportunities Party are finally seeking to break the deadlock on welfare thinking with a policy proposal of a UBI (universal basic income) for the over sixty-five-year-olds and the families with young children.[6] Morgan's broader thinking on this topic requires fundamental tax reform too.[7] Revolution is not impossible. We can create a welfare system that doesn't dehumanise real people and eradicate culture, relieves need, enables participation in our society, and doesn't bankrupt us in the process.

There's a scene near the beginning and at the end of *Mad Max: Fury Road.* If you haven't seen it, all you need to know is that this is a movie set in a post-apocalyptic world. There are many lovely, boganistic and physically impossible car chases and gory deaths. The movie is bookended with the same scene. The people who hold power in the citadel of this wasteland are in control of the only source of water. In the first scene, the nasty horrible tyrant releases a massive waterfall to his enslaved people to show he is in control. A petty water-hogging god. The cataracts of fresh water engulf the teeming, filthy, and parched crowd below, who fight each other to hold up their tiny basins and buckets to catch just the merest dribble of the flow.

At the end, the same waterfall is released, only this time, by the *good* people – the ones who have taken over the corrupt system. In both scenes, the huge flow runs into sand and away from those who so clearly needed it. It made me think of the difficulty of creating true change in our welfare system. Changing the people in the citadel is not enough if the mechanism of allocation remains effectively the same.

Bad Laws Sometimes Deserve To Be Broken

JULY 2017

In the opening moments of the 1970s, my father left my mother and followed his elusive business dreams to Australia. I have read several letters between the two of them, hurt and angry exchanges, and in all of them she asks him for financial assistance to raise their three children. He sent her a few payments, and eventually the letters and payments ceased. At some point my mother went on the new Domestic Purposes Benefit for sole parents (well, new in 1973). She stayed on that benefit until I left school, and then she shifted to the DPB woman-alone benefit, and on to superannuation. She was a beneficiary for about forty-one years.

During that whole time, my mother remained alone. She had offers of marriage but turned them down, in part because she did not want to be beholden to richer men. Ironically, the state support represented independence for us, despite all the rhetoric about reliance on benefits creating soul-suckingly dependent beneficiaries. My mother taught me about fighting for independence precisely *because* she was a beneficiary. She did not have to find succour from or be exploited by other people, just to survive.

I grew up watching her account for every one-cent and two-cent piece in our household budget, writing in little notebooks that, over decades, grew to fill drawers in the wall unit in the smoke-yellowed dining room. (And, yes, she was a beneficiary who smoked, and drank, and we never went hungry. Okay?) She earned extra money by taking in boarders.

Our mother was deeply concerned to ensure she never overstepped her earning boundaries, and that she never found out where our father had gone, after those early letters stopped coming. That was so she could honestly report on the benefit forms that she did not know where he was. I clearly remember her actually putting her hands over her ears at one point just so she could not hear us discussing where he was living. 'Sydney somewhere' was the most specific fact she allowed herself to learn about him.

In the 2017 pre-election period, dominated as it is by partisan breast-beating over the speeches, actions and inactions of Metiria Turei, some people might be tempted to use my mother's story of law adherence as some kind of moral lesson and counterpoint to Metiria's.[1] Don't. She was not a beneficiary saint or sinner. She just was who she was. No paragon or flag-bearer for anyone or anything. Her status as a beneficiary neither enhances nor degrades her moral character any more than her driver's licence did.

She chose to adhere to the laws of benefit eligibility. And I wonder if it might have cost her dearly to stay alone, as she did, until her death in 2015. She was a gregarious person who shunned many relationships and became quite isolated in her later years. I'll never know whether she might have been different had she not considered herself bound by such laws.

The only usefulness of putting her story in the public arena may be to prompt discussion about change. Her story is not an end in itself, and never should be. One further thing: it highlights that the relevant laws in her case have, from their very inception, been doomed to be broken.

Well, to be honest, that is a pretty trite statement. Every law exists only because someone out there will want to break it and do the thing she's not supposed to do, or fail to behave in the way she *is* supposed to.

But humour me ... and forgive me if you have heard this one before. Instead of looking just at the end result of a given law, it helps to see why it exists in the first place.

In our heavily targeted benefit system, widows' benefits and domestic purposes benefits uphold the long-standing social presumption that a husband will, as the primary breadwinner, support his wife and children in the usual nuclear family formation. To be eligible to get a benefit under the Social Security Act 1964, therefore, an applicant must not *also* be receiving significant financial support from someone else standing in for the missing husband. Applicants must be effectively *unsupported* if the state is to provide that missing support and effectively 'step into the shoes' of the absent husband, or the person who *should* be providing such support.

The gender-based language has gone, but the 'absence of support' requirement remains. Widows, single people, formerly married people, formerly de facto people, must now all be in the same unsupported boat to be eligible for sole parent support (now under s20D of the '64 Act, formerly known as the DPB sole parents' benefit).

If these people do get into a new relationship, they must not cross the line into emotional commitment and financial interdependence with another person. To do so would mean they are receiving *support* from that person. If they do, they must inform the state of that change in circumstance, be income-tested and accept the consequences, including the probable loss of the entire benefit.

And, even if eligible, these people can lose some of their benefit if they fail to, or refuse to, name the other parent or file for a child support assessment under the Child Support Act 1991. And if you thought that was some new neoliberal rule, ah nope. It has been around since at least 1936, and even earlier, when some deserted wives were able to claim a widow's benefit provided they could not find the husband who deserted them, and they filed for the earlier equivalent of child support.

Effectively these prohibitions uphold a general rule against *resource-pooling*, designed to ensure that no-one is better off with state support than others would be without it.

In my view these rules shepherded or perhaps forced my mother into a solitary life that I don't think she really wanted. In many ways she was acting *against* what we as humans usually do. Regardless of financial circumstances, people try to create bonds and relationships with others. We are social and we need each other. Yet compliance with the laws in this kind of case sets up a stark choice for the sole parent:

- Live alone with no substantive contact with a romantic partner that crosses an imaginary line into emotional commitment and financial interdependence, and accept support from the state,
- or enter such a relationship and lie about its existence, accepting support from the state,
- or confess the relationship and lose eligibility.

An invidious choice.

I have been amazed by the extraordinary rhetoric that has swelled in the wake of Metiria Turei's politically driven account of her own circumstances in the early 1990s. In particular, there has been a broad presumption in the public discourse that the laws that applied are either morally good or morally bad and that by breaching or adhering to such rules people like Metiria and my mother somehow reveal their moral character.

Sometimes morality and law does coincide and it is right that we should punish or promote certain behaviours as a society, if only to discourage others from doing bad things or to encourage others to do good things.

But let's not fool ourselves that any law is a guide to the human heart.

I generally try not to kill people. That may reveal that I'm not a habitual murderer, but says nothing else about who I am. I regularly break other kinds of laws, or regulations. Over the years, I have smoked and ingested drugs, I have trespassed, driven carelessly, assaulted people, sat on a kai table, used obscene language in a public place, walked over someone's legs in a wharenui, and transgressed all sorts of lines of decency. I'm sure the list goes on and on. My mother used to get me to buy her alcohol and cigarettes after school. I'm pretty sure she wasn't supposed to do that.

Not one of us leads a life in which we break no law.

By the same token, there is no point in pretending that any law is *neutral*. Laws are created in their cultural and political context. This context doesn't make the laws moral or immoral, but can lead to consequences that enforce a particular societal structure or view of that structure. The benefit laws reflect a presumption that people live in nuclear families and can therefore struggle to deal with the notion of whāngai (Māori adoptions), for example. While the laws prohibiting resource-pooling *appear* gender neutral, they are enforced primarily against women and far more rarely against men.

Māori are well aware of the oppression of seemingly ordinary laws that undergird the structure of a society that was never designed with Māori in mind. We ought not forget that Māori survival and social progress in this country has depended in part, at least, on Māori flouting laws; such as pulling up survey pegs, or occupying land that laws said were no longer theirs, holding so-called illegal protests, and the like.[2] We owe our law-breaking tūpuna a debt of gratitude, in many cases.

Nor am I drawing a false analogy between politically necessary law breaking by some in important parts of our history and the actions of genuine benefit fraudsters. I'm not a fan of benefit fraud (for example), and there are people who have been rightly punished for it. But there is merit in identifying where laws can set people up for inevitable failure, or have, with the passage of time, created social problems that can only be solved with sufficient political will.

I think our heavily targeted, morally directive welfare system is replete with laws that encourage failure, non-compliance and moral self-absolution. We need policies that will incentivise law keeping rather than law breaking. Let's discuss those possibilities.

And we don't need to be distracted by the storm of moral one-upmanship that helps no one and clarifies nothing.[3]

Te Puea Marae, Tūhoe and the State of (Māori) Welfare

JUNE 2016

It was the radio report that did it for me, and the tears flowed.[1] A young woman (named 'B' in public) and her whānau were farewelled from Te Puea Memorial Marae, after several days of staying there. Their plight caught national attention because B is a cancer patient and the family had been forced to move to Auckland from Hamilton for B's treatment, staying with family and friends because no affordable housing was available.

Why did I weep? I wept, not only out of compassion for that whānau and the hardship they have been through, but also out of pride. Te Puea Marae had extended to this whānau true manaakitanga, and when the family left the other day to move into a brand new state house, they were farewelled with a poroporoaki. There was kōrero, song, prayer, and tears. Listening to the account, my heart was full. Tikanga Māori and bloody hard work by the family and the volunteers, and social service providers (including WINZ), had shown the meaning of manaakitanga, and the rangatiratanga of this whānau had been upheld without bureaucratic interference.

To explain (if you didn't already know!). Te Puea Memorial Marae in Māngere decided in May 2016 to open up to the public in response to a perfect storm phenomenon in Auckland.

One storm has been house prices in Auckland increasing by nearly 80 per cent in five years, hiking rents in the process and forcing some already vulnerable families into overcrowded bedrooms and garages, or in some cases, out of homes entirely and into cars, or worse.[2]

Another (related) storm has been the decline in available affordable housing, due in large part to the growth of investor-based house purchases, and lack of homes being built sufficient for the growing population. One estimate, based on 2013 Census data, reckons 10,000 houses that could have served to help accommodate Auckland's growing population have simply not been built.[3]

Arguably, another storm has been the relatively high levels of estimated disengagement or lack of engagement of those in need of housing assistance with the Ministry of Social Development; up to 41 per cent of homeless recently surveyed had not engaged with MSD about housing needs.[4]

So, in May 2016 all of these storms converged, and B, her whānau, and all the whānau and individuals staying at Te Puea were sheltering from this combined ferocity. Te Puea Memorial Marae, by opening its doors, and setting up its Manaaki Tangata programme, took voluntary responsibility for the welfare of 'the people' at least to the end of August.[5] The marae's vision of who 'the people' are is not exclusive, but it places Māori at the top of the list, according to marae chair Hurimoana Dennis.

There is another, broader aspect to this story that demands attention. What Te Puea is doing (and other marae and entities around the country that are beginning to follow its example, including Manurewa Marae) is arguably fulfilling, at least in part, the role of the welfare state.[6] Too grandiose a suggestion? Perhaps not when seen alongside other recent developments, as well as in historical context.

After all, the work being done by Te Puea Marae is at one level extraordinary, and at another level completely ordinary. Māori seeking to provide welfare for Māori in a Māori way is a very old story. Even at Te Puea Marae itself, this is hardly new, although the added residential element has created a more intense dynamic.

> Kaanga Skipper, marae board member and direct descendant of Te Puea Herangi who the marae is named after, said Te Puea helped many people in the community when she was alive and would be happy at what they were doing.
>
> 'I believe when she put the pou into the ground she put me in the ground to make sure I would be available and be here to carry on with the work that she has done.'[7]

There are countless examples of structures, organisations, rōpū, councils and committees set up from the 1840s to the present day by Māori to provide welfare for poor Māori. Often this was necessary because Māori were not considered suitable recipients for charity, and land ownership was assumed to suffice as a resource base upon which Māori could survive. The later decades of the nineteenth century put paid to that notion for many Māori communities, but official discrimination against Māori based on that presumption would last well into the middle twentieth century.

The Kīngitanga had, even at its foundation in the mid-nineteenth century, the notion of Māori as the dispossessed poor, soon to be reliant on the system and aid of others. While preventing land loss was its primary focus, welfare was inextricably linked with that focus. Māori had become like fish, caught from the sea, and left to dry; maybe to be reliant on the aid of foreigners. In 1858 Wiremu Tamihana provided the following translation of part of Taranaki chief Te Akerautangi's speech in debating the installation of Potatau as Māori king:

> Welcome O King; welcome to Waikato.
> The shame I feel is great
> For thou hast made a hapless exit.
> And now thou art as fish caught from the sea
> And placed upon the stalls to dry;
> Are we to feed upon the things that come
> From lands far distant?
> O son, thou gavest this to me
> And caused these lips to be polluted
> Which once were sacred. Lo, I'll lop it off.
> Lest it should lead me to adopt its measures.[8]

Crucial to the idea of providing for Māori welfare was to possess or access sufficient power to make decisions about Māori welfare. Some initiatives sought to establish Māori governance bodies; for example, Māori councils were established under legislation in 1900 to enable Māori to make rules about, and attend to, what was understood to be local welfare needs. Māori MPs such as Sir Apirana Ngata sought to operate within government to achieve Māori welfare through rural land development schemes. But as Māori became separated from land, concepts of welfare shifted somewhat from dependence on land to urban-based support from the 1950s. Māori shifted activities accordingly, creating urban-based cooperatives, such as the Māori Women's Welfare League in 1951.

Many of these initiatives proved an extraordinary testament to the drive of Māori communities to cooperate with the government, but to solve their own welfare problems. As one shining example, the Māori War Effort Organisation (MWEO) morphed from a tribal-based entity intended to facilitate and encourage Māori recruitment for the Second World War into an extraordinarily successful welfare organisation that had unparalleled reach into Māori communities. An attempt to bureaucratise and centralise the MWEO and capture its success as a part of the Native Affairs (later Māori Affairs) Department undermined the success of that original entity, but led eventually to the establishment of the current New Zealand Māori Council and its district Māori committee system.

Bear with me, we'll be back in the twenty-first century soon ...

And by 1966, thirty-three such committees had been established in Auckland alone, taking on tasks such as mediating landlord–tenant relationships, providing budgetary advice, undertaking prison work, overseeing Māori wardens, establishing urban marae and carrying out a host of other activities merely labelled 'welfare work'.

Sound familiar?

One of the marae established in Auckland during this fertile period was Te Puea, named of course for the redoubtable Tainui leader Te Puea Herangi, who popularised the Kīngitanga and established many marae, prime among which was Tūrangawaewae at Ngāruawāhia. Her greatest fight, which she continued all her adult life, was against Māori poverty.[9]

One remarkable thing, aside from the work that Te Puea Marae has done and does now, is that mainstream New Zealand might actually think this focus is new, or unprecedented. If that is the case, that would only go to show how far Māori have been identified in the national eye with being both poor *and* terminally helpless.

Much of this misperception (if indeed it is such, and not merely a figment of my imagination) can be sheeted home to the monolithic power of the idea of the welfare state. Although the welfare state, engendered in 1938, deliberately excluded and underpaid Māori for decades on the presumption that Māori were too communistic and simply not cut out for citizenship, Māori have over the decades become the *nonpareil* subjects of the welfare state. Of course, as Māori lost land, whānau connection, economic footing and social standing, this identification with welfare was probably inevitable, but has handily erased other powerful versions of the Māori social narrative.

In short, many Māori have always had a vision of Māori welfare that establishes Māori solutions to Māori poverty. Is this a kind of separatism, as Lindsay Mitchell worries, alongside other luminaries of constitutional thought such as John Key?[10] I don't think so, because the equally powerful vision in Māori society is that of sharing in the common good with all New Zealanders.

In fact, it is this very tension between these two notions (rangatiratanga and sharing in the common good) that underpins a very relational Māori approach to citizenship. Māori communities have sought Māori solutions to welfare because we believe the relationship between Māori and the Crown guarantees us that space. The self-same relationship with the Crown guarantees us the same status as everyone else, with concomitant access to the common good. Both manifestations of this relationship can be easily traced to the Treaty of Waitangi.

Treaty settlements are beginning to reveal this interplay even more sharply, specifically in regards to welfare, and even more specifically in regards to our benefit system. As I wrote in a 2014 blogpost:

> The recent Tūhoe settlement [in 2014] includes a social services management plan whereby the iwi works in partnership with Crown agencies to deliver better social services to Ngāi Tūhoe. Interestingly, Tāmati Kruger made the following statement in April [2014]:

> ... under mana motuhake, the iwi plans to take responsibility for the estimated $9 million of benefit money distributed to Tuhoe annually. As part of the 40-year plan, the tribe will take state funding and use it change the dependency culture.
>
> Kruger said: 'We want to work with the Ministry of Social Development in utilising the $9 million of benefits to use some of that for job creation, and also changing a mindset in Tuhoe around being beneficiaries of the state.'[11]

This plan is in development, on the government side.

At the end of 2015 a report was made public on the MSD website. MSD commissioned the report by Sapere Research Group to explore the possibilities of devolving Crown liability for social security on to Tūhoe.[12] This was an exploration of possibilities rather than the formulation of a set plan, and is certainly not indicative of Crown policy. However, the very fact that these possibilities are being debated and floated is important, and these discussions must be monitored and kept public.

In my view, relational citizenship, as practiced by Māori, results from maintaining balance between seeking common benefit, or common good for all, and upholding rangatiratanga.

And I have a few warning bells ringing in my mind.

According to this report, MSD is currently working on measuring the actuarial liability of the Crown for Tūhoe's long-term welfare costs (in line with the investment approach). One of the more interesting parts of this 'think piece' takes its shape from a question the report writers were asked: 'We have been asked specifically by MSD as to how we would 'sell the liability' and, more specifically, if you wanted to 'sell' some of the [welfare] liability to Tūhoe, how would you do it?'[13] Wow. Once we can put a price on 'welfare', anything is possible. One suggested model for 'selling the liability' could be:

> Partial fiscal decentralisation. Under this option, the individual rights of the beneficiaries would be changed – or provision for an opt-out made – so that a calculated sum of money would be allocated to the Tūhoe to meet agreed social and economic objectives but with a degree of freedom to be negotiated for the Tūhoe to spend these funds more effectively than under the present centrally-managed system. Reasons for doing this would be to honour the relevant aspect of the settlement agreement, but also because it would be believed that the Tūhoe could get better results from the money because of the knowledge, proximity and influence with the potential beneficiaries.[14]

There is a lot of water to go under the bridge yet. Tūhoe has not been consulted on these ideas, because they have (according to Sapere) required the Crown signatories to the Services Management Plan first to expend the resources to carry out these investigations. It could be years before the shape of the Tūhoe solution to Tūhoe welfare is made public.

But it's important to be aware that these are the kinds of directions being explored, with massive implications for the notion of a single welfare state. Whatever direction is chosen, if the relationship between any iwi in Tūhoe's position and the Crown (in regards to welfare) is 'divested' too far, the iwi could be the ones to suffer.

The same may be said for the work being done by Te Puea and other marae in the urban context. Here's hoping the balance does not tip too far.

The Long Shadow Over Our Marae

NOVEMBER 2017

The kuia and I trade calls, our voices wreathed in the morning mist. The house before me, rooted in the earth, pushes up against the grey sky, creating space for us. The group advances with me. We pause. I remember my mum – two years passed. Her throaty chuckle echoes in my mind. Tears fall, again. We move on across the marae ātea.

The last of the calls fade into the air, and we shuffle into the house to find our place, our seats, trying not to be seen but still wanting to see. We negotiate parking spaces; we sit. We watch our breath floating on the air, we listen to the heat pump on the back wall straining to warm the winter void between carvings, weavings, people.

They sit, in the darkened corner, the four of them. An old, lean man with a piece of paper in his hands; a younger, slightly rounder man, both on the front bench. On the back bench sits the silver-haired kuia, smiling at no one in particular. The blonde girl perches off to the side. Knees pointing to the direction she really wants to take, as if she has been press-ganged into these cultural duties – while she was on her way to work, to her mate's place, to anywhere but here. Yet here she is.

Facing them, we sit. Our single speaker holds his smartphone in a tight grip; the words to his whaikōrero glaring from its tiny screen. Like me, he's been practising in the car on the way up. Women sitting around me hold pieces of paper, creases bisecting the words to our single waiata. In this pōwhiri it seems okay not to know things off by heart. No shame, but also little quarter given. What must be done must still be done, depletions and dwindlings be damned.

Tikanga, the Correct Way to Behave, carried us along in our willing conformity. Above all, the house holding us within it cannot be left to speak for itself.

Each kaikōrero stands and speaks as they must. As we all need them to. They pay just the right deference to God and gods, to land, to water, to sky, to us and to all our dead. Words ebb and flow between us, some of them in English. When the time comes, we join to harirū, to 'how-do-you-do'. Our twenty-five souls to their four. Us and our heavy footsteps on their marae and in their whare. Within the hour the four leave us, and we fill up their space with noise, chatter and our business.

In the two warmth-filled days I spent there it was hard to shake off the sense of foreboding I felt when I looked around me. It felt as if this place were under a shadow, ever-lengthening across our landscapes, falling over many of our marae.

More than 770 traditional marae complexes like this one, usually incorporating a wharenui or whare rūnanga (meeting house) and marae ātea (usually a clear space in front of the wharenui), are embedded across Aotearoa; at least 743 of them in the North Island. Dozens more pan-tribal complexes have grown in cities.

These documented structures don't tell the full story of our marae-claimed lands. Many of the traditional complexes are likely to be still unknown to researchers, given that there are more than 1,300 marae reserves registered under Te Ture Whenua Māori Act 1993.

Unsurprisingly, perhaps, these often-tiny built spaces are increasingly vulnerable to demographic change. As kaikōrero and kaikaranga in remoter areas decline in numbers, some paepae, or speaker's benches, are simply empty. In some places, too, the karanga is no longer heard.

We have known about this danger for a long time. My awareness of the lengthening shadow has been further provoked in recent weeks by a worrying series of events. A month or so after I returned from the marae hui, Bruce Stewart died at his beloved Tapu Te Ranga Marae in Island Bay, Wellington. An extraordinary man with a vision to match, Bruce left his people to remain as kaitiaki of an urban marae, hewn by hand out of recycled and scavenged materials, dug into the hillside.

Haere ki ōu mātua tipuna.
Haere, haere,
okioki ai …

That marae is also vulnerable, as a result of a fraught relationship with the Wellington City Council and with some in the community. Building compliance demands hang heavy on this idiosyncratic, ten-storey structure, described by council spokesman Richard MacLean as a 'death-trap'. Parts of the complex have been closed up and barricaded off from use.[1]

Almost a year before Bruce's death, his son Hirini acknowledged the shadow lying over their marae:

> It's the proverb he always told us – those who build the house are built by the house. And so all those people will come down with the house, if it comes down.

Well. We all have much to lose if our houses come down. The marae complex, no matter how plain, enables the iwi, hapū or urban collective to have a point of foundation in the world, by affirming the links of the people with ancestors, land, guardians and waters. The spaces of the marae ātea and the whare rūnanga make us cross thresholds: between the worlds of the living and the dead, between descendants and ancestors, between this world and other worlds. If such places can survive demolition, that is. For the very earth within which marae are embedded has been shifting and seething.

> Rū ana te whenua. Whati ana te moana …

From 1 July 2017, every wharenui or whare rūnanga has been counted as a 'building' under the newly amended Building Act 2004, unless it can show that it is a 'building used wholly or primarily for residential purposes'. Arguably, most marae whare are not usually wholly or primarily places of residence, so will likely have no exemption under the amended legislation.

Exemption from what, you ask?

Local councils will need to determine whether such 'buildings', including marae complexes, are earthquake-prone. If they are, the councils will issue notices requiring seismic work to be done by a deadline of the council's choosing. Given that at least 70 per cent of existing marae structures are estimated to be over fifty years old, the number of marae needing work done could be large indeed.

In brutal summary, marae deemed earthquake-prone will need to be upgraded or replaced, or face demolition. While marae complexes must be safe for all people, the potential financial, spiritual and emotional costs are likely to be huge, if not insurmountable, for poorer Māori communities.

In early 2016, the MP for Te Tai Tonga, Rino Tirikatene, unsuccessfully sought an exemption for marae under the Act, and tried to draw Parliament's attention to such complexes being more than mere buildings:

> [In] te ao Māori a wharenui is more than just a building. It is representative of our tūpuna. If we look at all the various parts of a marae, they are the parts of the body of our tūpuna, so there is more than just a bare-boned, inanimate-type object that we are referring to in this legislation. I think that is what this legislation fails to do – it fails to address the extra spiritual meaning that is applied to buildings.[2]

Other events have also prompted me to sense the shadow over our marae and their futures. During 2016 and 2017 there has been unprecedented coverage of the role of marae complexes as the providers of welfare and emergency assistance to anyone in need. Such media stars have included Takahanga Marae, which helped people after the 2016 earthquakes in Kaikoura, and Rautahi Marae in Kawerau, which opened its doors to flood victims after the April 2017 Edgecumbe floods.

There were Te Puea and Manurewa marae, housing the homeless in 2016 and 2017 as an emergency extension of government services in response to the housing crisis in Auckland. Marae complexes have become, more publicly at least, centres of emergency welfare. These activities push the marae beyond their usual functions.

In something of a cruel irony, the new building laws may stretch further too, to these marae. Councils will identify and prioritise 'buildings' likely to be used for emergency accommodation. Such buildings are more likely to be assessed earlier. If they are found to be earthquake-prone, such marae will be required to have the remedial work done more rapidly. Marae such as those I have just named could well be 'rewarded' for opening their doors to those in emergency need by being subjected to even greater scrutiny and earthquake compliance requirements than other buildings.

There was generous public praise of the marae which helped their communities in times of need. But praise is a fickle creature. During the same short passage of weeks in which Bruce Stewart passed and the new legislation was enacted, Awataha Marae in Northcote, Auckland, became the focus of an unprecedented political attack. The attack showed not only how Māori institutions and people can easily become political pawns, but also how marae can end up out of sync with their own communities.

In the run-up to the 2017 general election, the Labour Party established a scheme to attract young people from overseas to buy return tickets to New Zealand, so that they could participate for three months in an internship scheme that would give them valuable electioneering experience.

The scheme got too big for its boots, and the decision to house the interns at Awataha, an urban marae not designed for housing such a large number over such a long period of time, caused an outcry. Marama Fox, Māori Party co-leader, compared the interns to 'slaves'.[3] Some media described the marae itself, and the temporary sleeping structures it put up, as 'slum accommodation' and dubbed it 'the sweatshop marae'.

Although subsequent reports downplayed the culpability of the marae, mud sticks – and filth sticks even longer. The people of Awataha Marae faced reputational ruin over a situation for which they were largely not responsible. It is a well-known axiom among Māori that any marae that abuses visitors will lose its own mana and become dusty from its own neglect:

> Tangata takahi manuhiri, he marae puehu.

In fact, Awataha had already been the target of street protest weeks before the internship story broke. Some Māori, represented by Te Raki Paewhenua Māori Committee, felt excluded from the marae, which was designed to be used as an urban foundation point for local

Māori communities. They claimed that the marae was instead hiring itself out to other groups, severely limiting the use of the marae for tangihanga and other cultural celebrations and commemorations of local Māori. While it is anyone's guess how this long-simmering stoush will end, it is certainly true that a marae cannot, and perhaps should not, stand if the home people don't support it.[4]

The threat of disconnection between people and a marae leads me to yet another June 2017 event that forms part of the shadow in my mind's eye.

This time, the story occurs in Greystanes, Sydney, Australia. Three organisations — Ngā Uri o Rāhiri Inc., Te Aranganui and the Sydney Marae Appeal – had the dream of establishing a marae complex on leased land at the Hyland Road Reserve in Greystanes. Like all attempts to realise dreams, it took a lot of time, energy and fundraising – and then, at the last hurdle, the local authority, the Cumberland Council, rejected the proposal, seemingly without a backward glance. In the sometimes cruel and bloodless language of power that erases years of hard work, it was simply '[m]oved and declared carried by the Administrator that Council: 1. Abandon the current process relating to the proposed leasing of the subject land.'[5] The main reasons given were (broadly speaking):

- lack of sufficient cultural connection between the immediate area and the local Māori population
- issues of due diligence

- questions about the amalgamated groups' ability to fund the project.

Those backing the project disagreed. For now, at least, that dream sleeps.

This was not the only marae project in Australia. There's one in Melbourne, one in Western Australia, and probably others in the pipeline, too. It is hardly surprising, in a way, that such plans are afoot. From 2006 to 2011 the number of those recorded in the Australian Census as having Māori ancestry grew 38.2 per cent, from 92,912 to 128,434.[6] Historian Paul Hamer reckons that Māori in Australia now comprise at least 18 per cent of *all Māori*.[7]

Tā Mason Durie thinks that this kind of development was bound to happen. As he points out, there are already overseas marae. I presume that he is referring to places like Hinemihi in London, and the highly successful Aotearoa village at the Polynesian Cultural Center on Oahu in Hawai'i. It's just the next step in what Tā Mason calls 'sustaining the Māori Estate'.[8]

Marae have been constructed in overseas countries where significant Māori communities now reside, and as global travel increases, it is likely that overseas marae will be part of a worldwide network of marae, some based around hapū, others around communities of interest, and others still around global travellers who seek to retain a cultural anchor in an otherwise assimilating environment.[9]

And certainly Māori have spread overseas. For example, Māori have had a couple of centuries of deep connection with Parramatta in New South Wales. In 1811, while staying with Reverend Samuel Marsden, Ngāpuhi leader Ruatara established a small farm near the banks of the Parramatta River (originally the territory of the Burramattagal clan of the Darug people).

Marsden, having purchased the land, used the area to set up (briefly) a Māori seminary, supported by other Northern Māori rangatira such as Kāwiti Tiitua and Hongi Hika. This area is known still as Rangihou. Tūpuna are reportedly buried there, and if there were to be a place with a strong claim for a marae, quite possibly this is it. Accordingly, those trying to establish the marae at Graystanes sought to show connection between that project and those historical roots at Rangihou, a mere 8 kilometres away.

And, surely, setting up a marae complex deep in overseas soil can make sense, right? Maybe. Except ... it doesn't quite feel right. In particular, I wonder about the cost to the Indigenous peoples of Australia of Māori creating such permanent foundation points in that country.

I was astonished to find no mention in the Greystanes proposal's heritage report of the original Darug peoples of the area. While the proposal had the oral support of David Williams (of the Holroyd City Council Aboriginal and Torres Strait Islander Consultative Committee), a Bundjalung man from a different tribal area to the north-east of the Darug in New South Wales, there were no publicly available accounts of other Darug support for the proposal.

This absence of a Darug voice troubled me. I know that

my own knowledge is imperfect: perhaps those conversations never took place, perhaps they did. Regardless, the notion that marae complexes should be embedded in Australian soil disturbs me. When we dig into that soil to create places or points of belonging, no matter how well we think we have consulted with Indigenous peoples, that soil is not ours and will never be ours.

When I raised a similar issue recently, one woman responded by saying, 'Māori migrated to Aotearoa and built our marae there … never were we trees to plant ourselves in one spot. A marae is more than just the land it stands on.'

That's true. And we know from the settlement process that long-standing claims and cross-claims to land and mana whenua are still being quarrelled over today. But I don't think that history allows Māori or any other people to ignore and therefore to denigrate the peoples belonging to other lands that we would like to live on.

This doesn't mean we can't be Māori *on* that soil. How can we not be? We should guard and protect and develop our cultural expressions, even in little ways. But perhaps we should be careful to resist the tempting call to entitlement. Like birds drawn and fooled by the hunter, we might just end up in the pot.

E kore e rongo, he manu ka pakia pepetia.

The shadow that has troubled me over the past several weeks won't be going anywhere anytime soon.

Some of our marae are cold, and some of our houses have been left to speak for themselves. More will now struggle under the threat of earthquakes and the financial, spiritual and emotional burden of compliance, and the changes to tikanga such compliance might require. Urban marae are increasingly agents for social change and yet also pawns in political point-scoring, and some run the risk of moving beyond the reach of their own whānau.

And sometimes our people overseas are caught in the no-man's land between needing to be Māori, and needing to belong to overseas places, but being ever the manuhiri on the soil of others whom we should not supplant.

For many of us, the carved gate, the barely glimpsed tekoteko or the peeling paint on the side of what looks like a shed barely warrant another glance. Perhaps the very word 'marae' conjures up fond memories of a school visit in decades gone by. Perhaps these places only exist for us in the abstract, in the absence of an invitation across that threshold. For others of us, marae might reignite fears, memories of exclusion.

Regardless of our connections or otherwise, this marae-studded geocultural dimension of New Zealand society needs attention, protection, words and warmth. Like the language, marae may not survive as we currently know them, unless more of us tread them, sleep in them, call on them, fall in love in them, declaim and weep for them, and maybe even stump up our readies for them.

And thus, just maybe, we can push the shadow back.

Why Is God and Sexuality so Bloody Difficult?

APRIL 2018

Sometime after my thirtieth birthday, I gave in. All my life, there has been *something* I recognised, if I truly slowed down long enough to listen to the world around me.

Francis Spufford describes one of those moments of recognition in *Unapologetic:*

> It feels as if everything is with light, everything floats on a sea of light, everything is just a surface feature of the light. And that includes me. Every tricky thing I am, my sprawling piles of memories and secrets and misunderstandings, float on the sea; are local corrugations and whorls with the limitless light just behind. And now I've forgotten to breathe, because the shining something, an infinitesimal distance away out of the universe, is breathing in me and through me ... someone, not something, is here.[1]

And, despite the long and depressing history of colonialism around the world that I was very well aware of, and the torturous history of the relationship between Māori and the various Christian denominations that arrived in this country, I became a Christian that year.

Or, more accurately, I took my first wobbly Christian steps then. It is taking me many years to work out what being a Christian really is. I started attending an Anglican church, and there I remain.

Ah, church. The ultimate programming tool, right? Why bother? I could just go down to the beach to talk to God (whatever I perceive that to be) and feel good.

The god of sunny days, waterfalls, and puppies is not a very demanding atua. In fact, I can mould that kind of entity into anything I need it to be. I could have a permanent spiritual mascot with all the right political beliefs and all the right cultural characteristics, and I would always be right and never be wrong. My faith need never be on the 'wrong' side of any political, cultural, or moral issue ever again.

Why then choose a belief system that imposes any kind of orthodoxy, one not birthed in tikanga Māori, for example? The simple answer that any door-knocking God-botherer will tell you, is the Person of Christ, the guy who died on the cross and was resurrected, cracking the universe into 'before' and 'after'.

The framework is secondary to the Person. But without the framework, most of us haven't a chance of seeing the Person at all.

Actually, what many people, including many Christians, don't get, is that Christianity doesn't impose a rule book as such. No Leviticus memes to live by. No clean and unclean divisions of behaviour and objects. No 'good Christian' check boxes that we can fill in and then face the unknown future confident that we have Done What We Had To Do To Get In The Club.

Well, hang on. That's not quite true. There is a paragraph or so of stuff Jesus chucks out there that we *are* supposed to do, mostly cribbed from the Ten Commandments, but missing a few.

> 'You shall love the Lord your God with all your heart, and with all your soul, and with all your mind, and with all your strength.' (Mark 12:30)
>
> 'You shall not murder, you shall not commit adultery, you shall not steal, you shall not give false testimony, honour your father and mother,' and 'love your neighbour as yourself.' (Matthew 19:18–19)
>
> 'If you want to be perfect, go, sell your possessions and give to the poor, and you will have treasure in heaven. Then come, follow me.' (Matthew 19:21)

So really, it's all there in the last bit. We are to follow. To direct our feet and our lives, and our innermost beings, towards Christ. Along the way, we are to shuck off those things that would divert us from that journey. Apparently, that's how you become perfect.

Except following perfectly is bloody well impossible. Thanks, E Hoa.

According to the stories Jesus told, and the life he led, we have to give up those material things that matter to us, like status and money. Turn the other cheek to those who abuse us. Feed the hungry. Love the outcast. Forgive every bastard that does us wrong. Go after the sheep that has strayed. Risk everything for the child who has let you down and probably will do so again tomorrow.

And, above all, love.

And WE HAVE TO MEAN IT. There's no getting away with going through the motions, because the light behind everything knows us.

And so we fail.

And fail again.

And fail again.

Christianity is a religion of failures and dropkicks, hypocrites and losers, because most of us are good*ish*, but not one of us is good enough. We all know this regardless of belief, right?

Every one of us breaks things, be they relationships, promises, principles, or other people's bodies. On one level, admitting the truth of this is terrifying, and goes against everything we think we know in this modern world.

Our failure is not softened by our individual skill set and general awesomeness, nor by Tony Robbins or inspirational posters with sunsets and cats and little quotes that say things like: 'You are the best YOU you need to be right now!'

Self-improvement, while it can and does help us Do Life, will never mean we stop breaking things.

We will always break things.

But that hononga, that deep connection between all of us who break all the things, is also immensely comforting. We are never alone, thanks to the whanaungatanga of the f**ked-up.

We will keep breaking things and each other and we will still suffer. But if we keep turning back to God and acting accordingly, we are rescued from our broken state again and again. And we are loved no matter what.

But Israel Folau reminded us that Christianity includes the notion of judgment.[2] Furious struggle over what *counts* as brokenness ('sin') and as turning back to God ('repentance') and as following Christ ('righteousness') has caused, among us inadequate humans, exclusion and bigotry and countless deaths over many centuries.

Sexuality, cultural practices, cultural autonomy, the rights of women to their own bodies, the rights of slaves to freedom – all of these things have proved, and still prove, to be battlegrounds. Human sexuality is just the most recent of these.

At one level, judgment is pretty easy to understand. We do it all the time ourselves, discerning what is the right thing from the not-right thing. We can only 'judge' something properly when we know enough about that thing or that action.

I am judged right now by God because I am utterly *known* right now. There will also be judgment to come. I don't know what that looks like. But now, or then, everything I am is *known*, good and not – regardless of my careful construction of who I would rather the world see 'me' to be, that construction that secretes away my overuse of porn many years ago, my tendency to lie to myself, my subterranean arrogance.

It doesn't matter what that 'thing' is. What matters is that it draws me away from following Christ.

One of my favourite passages that explains how our 'things' get in the way between us and God comes from *Jane Eyre*. This nineteenth-century novel by Charlotte Brontë is often thought of as a simple, if wonderfully told, love story. You know, poor smart girl meets rich man with a dark past, they fall madly in love, and are about to tie the knot when she discovers he had a wife locked up in his attic all along. As you do. She flees, and realises in retrospect that her obsessive love for her would-be husband was the problem:

> My future husband was becoming to me my whole world; and more than the world: almost my hope of heaven. He stood between me and every thought of religion, as an eclipse intervenes between man and the broad sun. I could not, in those days, see God for His creature: of whom I had made an idol.[3]

Heterosexual love here was the broken 'thing'. Jane and Mr Rochester did eventually marry, once they got each other off their idolatrous pedestals and put God back in the centre of their lives together. (Don't hold your breath for this aspect of the story to appear in any *BBC* production).

So is homosexual practice itself one of those 'things' that prevent any person from living a Christ-following life? The short answer is of course it can. *Anything in the human condition* that may be bad, benign, or even a positive good, can morph into 'an eclipse [that] intervenes between man and the broad sun.'

'Ah!' say the eagle-eyed scriptural traditionalists, 'you are copping out. What about Romans 1:26–7 and 1 Corinthians 6:9–11?' Indeed. We can't gloss over these kinds of passages or wish them away, although there are way more passages condemning poverty.

The Romans reading looks back to the old story of the cities of Sodom and Gomorrah as the quintessential story of Screwed-up Humans Who Lost the Plot And Forgot God:

> (24) Therefore God gave them up in the lusts of their hearts to impurity, to the degrading of their bodies among themselves, (25) because they exchanged the truth about God for a lie and worshipped and served the creature rather than the Creator, who is blessed forever! Amen.
>
> (26) For this reason God gave them up to degrading passions. Their women exchanged natural intercourse for unnatural, (27) and in the same way also the men, giving up natural intercourse with women, were consumed with passion for one another. Men committed shameless acts with men and received in their own persons the due penalty for their error.

Verse 24 is the important one, actually. The sexually immoral behaviour *stems from* the worship of the creature (themselves) instead of the creator. The behaviour is a symptom of wrongness, not the cause.

So what about the Corinthians reading:

> (9) Do you not know that wrongdoers will not inherit the kingdom of God? Do not be deceived! Fornicators, idolaters, adulterers, male prostitutes, sodomites, (10) thieves, the greedy, drunkards, revilers, robbers – none of these will inherit the kingdom of God. (11) And this is

> what some of you used to be. But you were washed, you were sanctified, you were justified in the name of the Lord Jesus Christ and in the Spirit of our God.

Drunkards, thieves, and those who pursued sexual immorality in all its forms are to be treated the same. Sexual immorality was a big deal for Jesus, too. Merely *looking* at someone, wanting to commit adultery with that person, is enough to knock you off the path (Matthew 5:27–28). He never mentioned homosexuality, but he made his position clear – sexual immorality would *get in the way* of those who follow Him.

Many orthodox Christians, I think, would probably say that there is, in these verses, a clear condemnation of homosexual practice, even though it's no more serious or trivial than any other behaviour. Being habitually drunk is just as sinful. Therefore, homosexual practice (and by extension, for many, homosexuality itself), in this view, is one of those 'things'.

For me, though, the question is not 'what are the forbidden behaviours we must not do?' Remember, this is not a rule book.

Perhaps it would be more fruitful to identify the sexual behaviours that bring us *closer* to God. We know covenantal relationships do – marriage, for example – because they place Christ at the centre of the relationship. Sexual practice within the context of truly covenantal relationships then becomes rightly irrelevant.

The very notion of the possibility of same-sex covenantal relationships is relatively new (in the context of a 2,000-year-old religion), hard, and confronting. And one day it will need to be faced, despite the existence of Matthew 19, Jesus's condemnation of adultery:

> Have you not read that He who made them at the beginning 'made them male and female,'(5) and said, 'For this reason a man shall leave his father and mother and be joined to his wife, and the two shall become one flesh'? (6) So then, they are no longer two but one flesh. Therefore what God has joined together, let not man separate.

Traditionalists assert that all arguments end here. Marriage simply cannot be between men or between women. On this view, God cannot 'join together' same-sex couples. 'Nuff said.

The Anglican Church in 2014 affirmed that traditional definition of marriage. And yet, the 63rd General Synod (flash word for church parliament) of the Anglican Church in New Zealand and Polynesia, decided to allow for the blessing of same-sex relationships in New Plymouth in May 2018.[4]

The vote is not about allowing gay couples to marry in a church. That debate for now is closed.

What was decided was to allow church blessings of gay relationships in this corner of the worldwide Anglican communion. To cut a long story very short, a recommendation was made that bishops may authorise the use of 'a service blessing the relationship of two people, regardless of their sex or sexual orientation where the minister has satisfied him or herself that the relationship is loving, monogamous, faithful and the couple are committed to a life-long relationship'.[5] Nothing about this blessing will be compulsory for Anglican clergy. The rights of members to take different positions on same-sex relationships has been preserved.

Nevertheless, and regardless of the definition of marriage, this is a clear step towards recognising that all couples can enter into covenantal relationships, and therefore that sexual orientation and sexual practice are not merely, by definition, 'things' that get in the way of the journey to follow Christ.

It is fair to say that people were torn. And some walked away, and may yet still walk away from our communion.[6] The 85 million-strong Anglican Church worldwide will probably experience some degree of schism as other countries wrestle with the very same issue.[7]

And we, the equally broken, will continue to break ourselves and each other, until we return to the road we must travel, and whatever that requires of each of us.

Ka aru mātou i a te Karaiti
Tui, tui, tuituia mātou
Tuia ki te tumanako
Called to follow Christ
Bind us together
Bind us in hope.

In the Waiting Place

APRIL 2015

Are there any such things as ghosts of those who still cling to life, I wonder? I feel my mother here in her house, the house where I grew up. I hear her, beyond the range of my real hearing, moving about the house, softly. Carrying her hot water bottle up to bed. Moving softly outside to feed the birds, the creak upstairs must be her on her way to the loo, probably clutching the ever-present transistor radio. I hear the oven door closing. I can smell her too, or at least, the tobacco smoke, that ever-present blue haze, accompanied by the hacking cough. I can sense her sitting at the dining room table ruminating over the crosswords, adding items to the shopping list, keeping up with the diary. Cackling quietly to herself over some absurdity in the paper. I hear the shuffle of the spindly wooden chair as she stands on tiptoe to peer over the top of the fence onto Papanui Road for the latest local outrage to get her juices flowing. She always watches The Road. The missing recycling bins, the occasional vandalised letterboxes, and the sniffy reproachfulness of Her Next Door, who (apparently) everybody round here loathes. The Road is a living stream of cars, people, dogs, bikes, news, and the rumbling buses belching their payload of gritty exhaust fumes, mimicking little earthquakes that nobody needs. And then there is her little green oasis nestled between the house and the fence. The place where the birds come to feed and talk. The broken birdbath, the dishes with honey water and the containers with bread scraps. I can hear her 'took-took'ing to the birds. Not those bloody starlings though. No truck with those bloody bullies. Wax-eyes, sparrows, fantails ... and before the earthquakes, the hedgehogs. We wonder where the little hedgehog family went to, four years ago. She misses them.

I am sitting here at 2 a.m. in the morning and I am waiting for the bang of the poker on the floor upstairs to let me know it's time to Turn That Bloody TV Off. I'm waiting for the turn of the handle of the door into the hallway and for her to drift into the room on her way to put the kettle on. She's going to be pretty mad. Never the tidiest of people, I have let the lounge in which I am camping turn into, well, a freedom camper's paradise. Minus the poo, at least.

So I can hear all these things and see them all too, if I close my eyes and block out the *Emmerdale* marathon on TV. But she isn't here, and she never will be again. At least, I don't think so. Not until she lies here and we gather for her.

My mother is sleeping fitfully, no doubt, a few streets over, at the Home Hospital. Her mind and body wander now, and she is waiting for the close of this chapter. I'll go back tomorrow to sit with her. I'll marvel anew at the kind of ethereal beauty that has come upon her recently as she slips just a little further away from us. She slips in and out of this world and then she'll blindside me with her wit and knowingness. And then she's off again into a world we can't really enter. Her knees are enormous. That's what happens when the flesh disappears from every other part of her body. Joints become bulbous.

Smoking, the one thing that gave her The Passenger, as she calls her tumour, the one thing that put her in hospital last month and into twenty-four-hour end-of-life care this month, is also the thing that gives her days rhythm, her movements purpose. The crosswords and diary sit unfilled, except by us, her children, as we try to fill in the gaps, perhaps to hold out to the world that there is still continuity with that old life. Twice a day comes the pilgrimage, the slow wander with the walker, or lately, the wheelchair, to the scruffy green patch with the tables and plastic chairs, where she lights her cigarette, breathes deeply, and sighs in contentment. The smoke floats around her like a deadly nimbus; but the irony still pinches. That one thing that put her here is the one thing that gives her any remnant of her own life now. She picked up her first cigarette at the age of fifteen in Eastbourne, about the time she left school and her parents divorced, around 1951. She thinks she pinched one of her dad's. Well, they all smoked. And now, she revels in the camaraderie of the shunned. She smokes out here with the staff and with a couple of the residents. She'll smoke alone if you let her, and the cigarette perches weakly between her fingers with the ash always threatening to drop onto her lap. The smoke wreathes me too, and I breathe it in.

The other day one of the new nurses joined us; a lovely young lady in her twenties. As my brother said later, she knows, surely, that my mother may be her future. If so, she gives no sign, just her kind smile.

So much kindness at that place. When she had a terrible pain break through the slow-release morphine fug yesterday, our mother wept, and her eyes were wide with fear. I pressed the call-button willing my own tears to stay inside, and within seconds the nurses were there, bustling, stroking, soothing, administering, watching. 'Don't scare me like that!' said one, not because the situation was beyond her ken, but because she just didn't want my mum to be in that terrible pain. Neither do we.

Well. Perhaps time to try and sleep again, before the tears burst out again and the sounds of my mother's not-yet ghost once again inhabit these quiet hours.

A Good Death

JUNE 2019

We all knew, as our mother got older, that she wanted the 'plug' pulled when the time came. In her view of the world, if she couldn't have a drink or a smoke under her own steam, as her saying went, it was time to go. Hers was a position of utter belief in the worth of independence and autonomy. Anything other than an independent life was not worth living. At the age of seventy-eight, robbed of her precious independence by lung cancer and dementia, she smoked her last cigarette in the smokers' yard at the Bethesda Rest Home and Hospital, and left us a couple of days later, in 2015. As I cleaned out years of yellowed correspondence from her house a few days after her death, there were dozens of newsletters from the End-of-Life Choice Society. I felt sad for my mum at the frustration of her beloved choice. I don't think she ever knew how utterly dependent she became, in the end. But then again, as I have written elsewhere, her tiny life at the end still had beauty in it.[1]

There is much to admire in my mother's stance on end-of-life choice, one shared with at least some of her friends. They wanted, and still want, the power and the right to determine their lives' ends. The scenario to haunt their dreams and to avoid at all costs is one of being tethered to machines, with life's pleasures stolen away and intolerable pain, all signalling the worst thing of all: utter dependence. The dependent life, in this view, is no life at all. There is a great value placed on the idea of freedom of choice. Its antithesis, the absence of choice, is something to be feared and avoided. In this thinking, giving the option of a chosen death is noble and compassionate; whereas allowing only an unchosen lingering death is ignoble and cruel.

Of course, there is much more to that debate.

There are all kinds of factors that play into the debate on assisted dying in New Zealand at present, lately manifested in response to David Seymour's private member's Bill, still awaiting its second reading at the time of writing.[2] Often, the entry into the debate is by way of stories. The story of Lecretia Seales and her fight in the courts to enable her doctor to assist her to die was compelling. There is no shortage of compelling stories that provoke our pity and fear for those caught up in those narratives, like that of Peter and Patricia Shaw, an Australian couple who killed themselves in October 2015.[3] Or the story of the terminally ill nine- and eleven-year-old Belgian children who have been the youngest to be euthanised in that country in 2018.[4] But a law on euthanasia needs more than the most compelling narrative.

I sometimes get asked what the 'Māori perspective' is on assisted dying. I can't pretend any expertise on this, or claim to speak for Māori communities. There are many perspectives, although only rarely expressed in the public domain.[5] However, some of those whakaaro have been reported by the Justice select committee on the End of Life Choice Bill. So I'll let the committee report back:

> Although not all submitters who identified as Māori oppose the bill or consider it inconsistent with Māori tikanga (values), others have several concerns.
>
> Submitters described a Māori worldview where people are part of their whānau, hapū, and iwi, where care, respect, and reverence are shown for the elderly and terminally ill, and life and wairua (spirituality) are valued.
>
> Some believe that assisted dying would breach the tapu (sacredness) of the person and have spiritual consequences for those involved. Some submitters consider that the bill would breach the Treaty of Waitangi. In particular, they cited the Treaty's underlying principle of tiaki (protection) of Māori values and, under Article 2, the concept of the taonga (treasure) of life.
>
> Other submitters consider that the bill would contravene holistic models of Māori health, such as Te Whare Tapa Whā, which sets out four equally balanced foundations of Māori health: physical, spiritual, family, and mental.[6]

It is possible to imagine an assisted death taking place in the context of a warm and loving whānau environment. The range of viewpoints suggest that Māori are not of one collective mind in regards to how tikanga Māori may or may not be at odds with the idea of assisted dying. However, there are pragmatic concerns of more urgency. Many of the submitters on the Bill were just as concerned that racial inequities already existing in the New Zealand health system will be magnified with the introduction of assisted dying:

> Some submitters believe that assisted dying would further contribute to discrimination and prejudice that already exists in the health system. They consider that Māori and Pasifika are less likely to be able to pay for health care, and that they receive lower standards of care and have less access to palliative care.
>
> Therefore, they believe these groups will be disproportionately more likely to request assisted dying than other groups.
>
> Submitters also believe that these groups are less likely to be treated by health practitioners of their own culture or those who understand their world view. They regard it as important that health practitioners understand the correct procedures for tāngata māuiui (sick people), their transition to death, and the treatment of tūpāpaku (the deceased).[7]

The position described above is supported by research by the Kia Ngāwari study (2010–12) funded by the Health Research Council of New Zealand, a study of twenty-seven whānau Māori, that reveals how important collective processes often are for whānau Māori at end of life, and how Māori are less likely to be able access sufficient palliative care. Rangatiratanga is vitally important for dying Māori too, but being able to *exercise* rangatiratanga fully means that whānau must be resourced properly:

> [T]he economic and material ramifications of colonialism impact on Māori hugely at the end of life, directly influencing the ability of whānau to identify and access much needed resources and palliative care support.
>
> Generally, only whānau who had a family member with a tertiary qualification or employment within a health or related field were well placed to identify and access much needed statutory support, palliative care and resources.
>
> Knowledge of the health system, or previous use of specialist palliative care services, increased the likelihood of some whānau accessing palliative care support and resources. When combined, these things strengthened whānau to provide the best care, frequently under difficult circumstances.[8]

One of the greatest questions about the prospect of assisted dying being enacted in New Zealand law arises because the proposed legislation establishes a process that presumes an individual can make a true choice to die. Many of the submitters opposed to Seymour's bill cite the problem of the *vulnerable person* being pressured or coerced to die by others. Dr John Kleinsman identified five types of vulnerability as an expert witness to the High Court in Lecretia Seales' case.

> *communication vulnerability*, represented by persons who are impaired in their ability to communicate because of distressing symptoms;
>
> *institutional vulnerability*, which refers to persons who exist under the authority of others;

differential vulnerability, which includes persons who are subject to the informal authority or independent interests of others;

medical vulnerability, which refers to those with distressing medical conditions; and

social vulnerability, which includes persons who are considered to belong to an undervalued social group.[9]

While Lecretia Seales absolutely denied that she was in any way vulnerable as described in any of these categories, whānau Māori with dying members are likely to fit into some or all of these vulnerability categories. As pointed out by Dr Hūhana Hickey, Māori are also more likely to be experiencing disability, and thus more likely to be considered vulnerable in that context as well.[10] And, as noted by the Disability Commissioner, the priority should be that disabled people are enabled to exercise the choice to live: 'Before the country legislated choice in death, it needed to work towards ensuring, to the greatest extent possible, all people had the same freedom of choice in life.'[11] In any event, what would be the *nature* of the choice to die for any person in any of these categories?

Often to be found at the very heart of our general Western legal system is the notion of the freely choosing individual, the individual-rights bearer. The person who, when faced with a choice of courses of action, is capable of choosing one of those courses of action. Such individuals must have free will in order to exercise a real choice; an idea that is powerful and optimistic. Thousands of years of philosophical and religious thought have also upheld this idea, particularly in the West – that humans can, for example, choose obedience to a deity or a principle, or a moral. Why not assisted dying?

At the heart of much opposition to the End of Life Choice Bill is a denial that *all* choice exercised under such legislation will truly be free. Those who oppose the legislation because of the danger it poses to vulnerable people will identify that there is no level of security the Bill can offer that will reassure them that the choice to die in every single case will be freely made. Those who cannot truly and freely choose should be protected by the state, not exposed to greater risk of death. An open letter signed by more than 170 lawyers put it this way:

> We believe that the mark of our civilised society is measured by the manner in which we treat and protect our weakest and most vulnerable members. While the Bill purports to be targeted to a 'small but significant group of competent adults who are not vulnerable and who wish to die without unbearable suffering and pain', we consider that it will in fact place many vulnerable members of our community (whether terminally or chronically ill, disabled or mentally ill) at greater risk of premature death by homicide or suicide as a result of neglect, coercion and other forms of abuse, as well as misdiagnosis or prognostic error and uncertainty.[12]

I would count myself in that camp. Well, I should do. I signed the open letter. At present, all that stands between a vulnerable person making a decision to die and the enactment of such a decision in the Bill, are a set of criteria. A qualifying person must be one who, on the current form of the Bill:

> (4) ...
>
> (c) suffers from –
>
> (i) a terminal illness that is likely to end the person's life within 6 months; or
>
> (ii) *a grievous and irremediable medical condition*; and
>
> (d) is in an advanced state of irreversible decline in capability; and
>
> (e) experiences unbearable suffering that cannot be relieved in a manner that the person considers tolerable; and
>
> (f) has the ability to understand –
>
> (i) the nature of assisted dying; and
>
> (ii) the consequences for them of assisted dying.

At present, to ensure coercion does not exist, the certifying medical practitioner must:

> 8 ...
>
> (h) *do their best* to ensure that the person expresses their wish free from pressure from any other person by —
>
> (i) conferring with other health practitioners who are in regular contact with the person; and
>
> (ii) conferring with members of the person's family approved by the person ...[13]

David Seymour, responding to submitters' concerns, has proposed significant changes, including deleting the option under s4(c)(ii).[14] In that case, only those facing a terminal condition would be eligible for assisted dying. He has also proposed strengthening the protection against coercion so that a certifying medical practitioner must be 'satisfied' that no coercion exists.

I suspect though that even with these changes, little will change between the entrenched positions of this debate. Few on this side of the maunga are ever likely to accept that *any* caution or protection that may be inserted in the legislation can ever bring about true protection of the vulnerable, whoever we conceive the vulnerable to be. For many, I suspect the opposition lies more deep than that and depends on a particular vision of humanity. We tend, I think, to divide into those two great camps: those for whom the idea of the autonomous individual is supreme, and those for whom human interconnectedness is the greater vision. The dividing line between these positions can be porous, it's true, but the camps exist, and don't neatly align with political concepts of left and right.

An additional and often unspoken factor in the public discourse is that many like me who have a religious faith have an understanding that we are dependent on what we conceive of as the Divine, as well as on each other, for our existence. This understanding of dependent existence will *always* make an assisted dying regime difficult (but not impossible) to accept.[15] For others, such a position can be utterly offensive and even a denigration of autonomous individual personhood.

My mother and I resided in those two different camps and respected each other's position. Perhaps the more salient point is that my brothers and I, because of excellent palliative care, were able to come together, in love, to accompany our mother to the veil at the close of her day. Equitable and free access to excellent palliative care and a good death, as far as it is possible, should be upheld by law and policy for each one of us. The truly terrible thing is that it is not. Assisted dying legislation represents an absence of hope that it ever will be.

[The End of Life Choice Bill passed its third reading on 13 November 2019 and, at a binding referendum held during the 2020 election, the Act was approved by a majority of voters. The provisions of the legislation will come into force in November 2021.]

The Empathy Gap and Me

DECEMBER 2018

A little while ago, I was driving a car down State Highway 1 and I was howling. Actually howling, snotty tears and all. Then I'd pull over for a bit, recover myself, move off again, and then something would catch in my throat. Then I'd be howling again.

Such car-cocooned moments are not unheard of for me in recent years. Ever since my mother died in 2015, I can get caught by grief, unawares, and find myself sobbing, or at least leaking, at traffic lights because something set me off. Last time that happened was when *RNZ* had the temerity to play Air Supply. It helps to have a supply of tissues at the ready.

These tears were not due to my mother on this occasion, though. I'd just left a house where a whānau had been sharing their history with me for a cultural report I was writing for a sentencing hearing that was coming up in the new year.

My howling was borne of inarticulate rage, and helpless misery that any family in New Zealand had to go through the utter trauma that they'd had to go through in their past and present. My hūpē and tears were never going to make a damn bit of difference to that whānau history, nor to the pain of the victim in that case, but they came anyway.

I think, too, there was some recognition that what they'd been through was not entirely disconnected to my own family history. I think some grief for our own family trauma was in there too – trauma far beyond my own direct memory. My empathy gap had been well and truly plugged.

It's easy to have an empathy gap. In fact, it's unavoidable.

By comparison, *compassion*, or the feeling of sympathy for others in misfortune, is, for many of us, not that difficult if we care to exercise it. And, of course, our society and its communities also suffer from a fairly healthy compassion gap, too.

But feeling compassion is probably less problematic, perhaps because compassion can be as much about what we *don't want to experience ourselves* as what we feel about the lives of others.

Empathy is slightly different, though. Empathy is understanding and sharing the feelings of another person. Perhaps, by definition, to empathise with another person we have to be able to feel what they feel. Perhaps we must have been through what that person has been through, or something similar, in order to empathise with them.

A lack of true empathy doesn't necessarily mean a person can't truly help another. Humans have resources to call upon other than just empathy. But it can help to understand a person well enough to be able to help in a way that makes sense.

Generally speaking, social welfare and criminal justice case-workers will usually (but not always) have some form of empathy gap between them and those they are supervising or processing or writing about – or judging.

This is not necessarily a moral failing. Many of us simply can't feel or imagine the life of another. We can't walk in their shoes. We might even lack the mental imagery and hardware to do it.

And although we can more easily feel for others – pity them even, if we allow ourselves to – often we can't truly understand them, if our lives haven't already somehow prepared us for that moment.

It's possible to learn empathy, but I think that would be hard. Not impossible, but hard. Moral failing, including racism, may exist in the refusal to try.

Or there's something more complicated. Sometimes we can bend over backwards to quash or deny our empathy for others. Merely sharing experiences is not enough. Sometimes we can view others only through lenses that just reflect us back to ourselves: 'I went through what she went through, and I turned out okay.'

Perhaps also, some Māori who've come from traumatic backgrounds may not want to empathise or have compassion for others with similar backgrounds.

Denied empathy is one thing, pretend empathy another. I remember years ago, as a twenty-something probation officer, having a young Pākehā guy come and visit me at the office. I was supervising him. But he didn't want to be there – he had better places to be.

I was trying to establish some kind of rapport with him. It was the uncertain start to another new relationship neither of us really wanted. I had some wise point to make (for his own good, of course) that I now forget. I leaned forward in my chair, keeping earnest eye contact, and said: 'Listen, mate ... ' as if I was going to impart something unprecedented to the lucky soul. He reared back as if I had spat in his direction. 'Don't call me *mate*! I'm not your bloody mate!'

He was right. I had presumed some kind of connection, but I was merely pretending that we were on the same team, that there was some kind of fellow experience between us. In short, I was trying to pretend that I empathised with him, and he called me on that bullshit.

I never forgot it. I try not to manufacture empathy. I try to feel it if I can, allow the seeds of it to grow, but I can't pretend it exists when it doesn't. Where it doesn't, I have to call on other things, my compassion and aroha, my instincts, and my morality.

How do we make connection and offer support or help that makes sense if we don't try to plug the gap?

I think what had happened, on that day in my car, was an upwelling of compassion but also the shock of empathy – which I hadn't been faced with for a while, for whatever reason. On the surface, this whānau's experience looked nothing like my own. Theirs was a story of extraordinary poverty both of love and money. An intergenerational story of gang affiliation and of repeated escape attempts. A story of loneliness, rejection, despair and some hope.

But, actually, that story had a similar point of genesis to my own whānau story. At the bottom of it all was war with the same enemies: land deprivation, urbanisation, fractured histories and self-loathing, leading to sexual abuse, violence, substance abuse and bad decisions.

Tempered, of course, by collective agency, individual resilience, ambition, sheer bloody-mindedness and some better decisions. We also shared a common Māoriness. We could lob the same words into our conversation, trusting each other to catch them. We knew some of each other's family names. We could follow an unspoken tikanga of how to speak with each other. We had never met. We were from different parts of these islands. And yet.

Thus, my empathy was not predicated entirely on a nice and chummy fellow feeling and understanding with another individual or two. It was predicated on the certain knowledge that my people's and their people's experiences were recognisable, connected, and of like substance.

Recent psychological research has suggested that there is such a thing as cultural empathy. We simply are more likely to empathise with those who are more like us than not. Well, duh.

That, and other experiences led me to question (as if any more questions are needed) the role of culture in criminal justice – in particular, the usefulness and role of cultural reports that can be called for at sentencing. After all, that was what I was doing in that family home that day: asking questions to write a cultural report.

I think I wrote a better report because of my empathy. That was of some help, I think. Small in context, but something.

But beyond that?

We all know the stats are bloody appalling. Within our criminal justice system generally and the prison population specifically, we know Māori are over-represented in comparison to the general population.[1]

According to the Ministry of Justice, in May 2018, the total prison population was 10,435. Māori made up 50.7 per cent of all sentenced prisoners in New Zealand, despite comprising just 17.5 per cent of New Zealand's population. Of all sentenced male prisoners in New Zealand, 50.4 per cent are Māori men, while Māori women now make up 63 per cent of all sentenced female prisoners.

An even bleaker and worsening position is occupied by Māori youth. Māori comprised 65 per cent of all youth in prison in 2017, up from 56 per cent a decade before.[2] There are now more than 5,000 Māori people in New Zealand jails.

This over-representation extends well beyond the jail cells into the experience of being a victim, the exercise of administrative and police discretion, charging figures, bail decisions and prosecution figures. We all know this by now.

That's where the reports do fit in. Parliament decided as far back as 1985 that such growing over-representation of Māori in the New Zealand prison population could, in some way, be addressed at sentencing, by way of the introduction of Section 16 of the Criminal Justice Act 1985 (now repealed).

That provision was originally enacted in order to encourage the use of alternative sentences to imprisonment.[3] However, the provision wasn't well understood by counsel or the judiciary, and as a consequence was completely underused.

Fast forward nearly twenty years and now we have Section 27 of the Sentencing Act 2002. This was built on the idea of the original Section 16 from 1985, and now allows judges to gain insight into the cultural backgrounds of all offenders generally.

But it can be used to focus on Māori offenders specifically, with the overall goals of reducing imprisonment rates and, like its predecessor, encouraging more use of rehabilitative and community-based sentences. Until recently, Section 27 has also been significantly underused.

Under Section 27(1) an offender due for sentence may request the court to hear any person or persons called by the offender to speak on the following matters:

(a) the personal, family, whanau, community, and cultural background of the offender
(b) the way in which that background may have related to the commission of the offence
(c) any processes that have been tried to resolve, or that are available to resolve, issues relating to the offence, involving the offender and his or her family, whanau, or community and the victim or victims of the offence
(d) how support from the family, whanau, or community may be available to help prevent further offending by the offender
(e) how the offender's background, or family, whanau, or community support may be relevant in respect of possible sentences.[4]

Note that this is not aimed solely at Māori, but there is no doubt that Māori over-representation was at the heart of the design of the section. Section 27 is part of a code that also relies on Section 8(i) in the Sentencing Act, which provides that the court *must* take into account 'the offender's personal, family, whanau, community and cultural background in imposing a sentence or other means of dealing with the offender with a partly or wholly rehabilitative purpose'.

Although an interpretation of Section 27(1)(b) on its face appears to require a causal link between the offender's *individual and specific* cultural information or background and the commission of the offence –'the way in which that background may have related to the commission of the offence' – interesting and very recent developments in New Zealand courts appear to echo Canadian approaches that simply don't require the demonstration of such a specific and individualised causal link.[5] Permission has been given to look further afield at systemic deprivation.

In particular, in a recent decision in the High Court case of *Solicitor General v Heta,* Justice Whata accepted that, while sentencing does not *on its face,* require any discussion of the systemic deprivation faced by Māori, the operation of Section 8 in combination with Section 27 of the Sentencing Act 2002 certainly *allows* for the court to hear such material.

An important thing to grasp here is that the Māori experience of colonisation, disease, war, urbanisation and deprivation is unique to Māori in this country, and is not shared with any other ethnic or cultural groups in the same way.

This realisation was part of what lay behind my tears on that road trip. We were alike in our culture, and part of that culture has been now recognised to include the intergenerational experience of trauma.

At long last, the courts are catching on, even if at a glacial pace, to what Tariana Turia was on about nearly two decades ago.[6] And now, with the release of *Every 4 Minutes*, a report on family violence, we have the Chief Science Advisor laying some of the impetus for family violence at the feet of the trauma of colonisation.[7]

We're beginning to understand that the modern experiences of Māori individuals can't really be fully explained by reference to one such individual's immediate and siloed history alone.

Of course, it's not enough for us to have the emergence of yet more reports, more bad stats, and cultural reports being used more often in the way they were intended.

Māori being sentenced to shorter sentences of imprisonment on the basis of fuller cultural information being brought before a judge is hardly going to change the world.[8] The young men and women who have cultural reports written about them aren't going to be walking into courtrooms where the inevitable empathy gap has magically been eradicated.

We can and must push for better information to be put before judges in sentencing. We can demand improvements to the Bail Act.[9] We can push for better programmes in prison, for more therapeutic jurisprudence, for something better than prisons. All of that.

But we can't expect institutions to be empathetic and compassionate to the thousands of Māori in the system now, and to the Māori children who are going to be sucked into it in the future. That is *our* job on a daily basis.

And, if we just can't find the empathy for whatever reason, then we use compassion, aroha, instincts, smarts, and all the rest to close the gap and keep our people out of the system.

Maybe then ...

Maybe then.

Teaching and Learning

OCTOBER 2019

I want to use words from Jeremiah as a leaping-off point:

> 'No longer will they teach their neighbour,
> or say to one another, "Know the Lord",
> because they will all know me,
> from the least of them to the greatest,'
> declares the Lord.
> 'For I will forgive their wickedness
> and will remember their sins no more.'

In the wake of the 2018 Census results recently released, we might be forgiven for feeling down about the fact that only about 38 per cent of New Zealanders profess Christianity. As some have observed, this may simply be because we are now more honest and less likely to report an affiliation to Christianity simply borne of habit or tradition. Either way, the words of Jeremiah speak to us now. We are again a country that more than ever needs our neighbours to teach each other, to help each other find the living bread, because most of us in our country simply don't know the Good News. Many of us in New Zealand think we know the fundamentals of Christianity because we see the symbols of it in our art, our languages, our storytelling, our shopping habits, but we really don't. For most of us, the Gospels, the Bible and the triune God it reveals to us are undiscovered country. It will remain undiscovered unless someone shows us the way.

Which brings us to the famous story of the death in 1836 of Tarore, a young Ngāti Hauā girl, and the eventual forgiveness by her father Ngākuku of her killer Uita of Ngāti Whakaue. This is a story I had never heard before becoming an Anglican, and I had never heard of Joy Cowley's telling of the story until a couple of years ago I think.

Much of what we know of Tarore's life and death descends to us from Ngāti Hauā oral tradition as well as from the journals of the Reverend A.N. Brown, who made a written record of the event and its immediate aftermath (which was then included in the 1838 select committee report to the English House of Lords on 'The present State of the Islands of New Zealand').

According to Dr Rosemary Dewerse, referring to Ngāti Hauā kōrero, Tarore had an extraordinary gift of memory: she had studied at the mission school in Matamata run by Charlotte Brown and had committed much of the Gospel of Luke to memory. Her father Ngākuku was himself a preacher of the Gospel, and in the early days Tarore would go with him and, when requested by her father, would quote from Luke to those assembled. This time was short-lived however, and in October 1836 the mission school at Matamata had to be closed and the children evacuated because of fighting between Te Arawa and Ngāti Hauā. It was in the process of the evacuation of the children from Matamata to Tauranga that they were attacked; Reverend Brown suggests this was in revenge for a man who had recently been killed. In any event, Tarore was killed.

Reverend Brown reports a direct conversation with her father on the day she died, where he said he was in darkness because he didn't know if she was in the Christian Heaven or whether she had gone to Te Rēinga. He said he knew that she had heard the Gospel, and that she could read it, and say it, but did not know if she had received it in her heart. This doubt is important for us to remember. The text is not magical, we do have to have it explained to us, we need teachers too. It cannot be right to build Tarore up as a mere symbol far beyond her human ordinariness. She was a real girl. Her own father was unsure if she really understood the Gospel. And she died, horribly.

In most tellings of the story, there is no active role for Tarore herself. Her great act is simply in dying; in martyrdom. Sometimes I think we almost fetishise her death, skating lightly over the utter wrongness and awfulness of it.

We know too that her death also has to be viewed in its own cultural context. Māori criminal law did and does not operate as a matter of individual fault as the Western system of criminal law does. And given our reservation in regards to sources, we may be able to see an echo of Māori criminal thought in the story, because Ngākuku does not immediately blame Uita. Reverend Brown reports that Ngākuku says to his own people: 'There lies my child. She has been murdered as payment for your own bad conduct.' This is consistent with what we know of Māori concepts of criminal liability. The collective entity Ngāti Hauā had failed Tarore by their own actions, perhaps of pursuing armed conflict with Te Arawa; theirs was the blame. That blame could be expiated in exacting utu, as a matter of collective agency. And it is this collective path that Ngākuku appears to reject when he is quoted as saying: 'But do not you rise up to obtain satisfaction for her. God will do that.'

This is an extraordinary shift in understanding; as a rangatira, leading his people in surrendering collective responsibility for utu to God. Just as extraordinary is Uita's later whakaiti or humbling of himself to join Ngākuku, and for the two of them to worship together. Yet it is what comes next that really ensured that story was preserved and handed down to us today.

One of the important moments of the story is that when Tarore dies, she is carrying a copy of the Gospel of Luke, and her killers, including a man called Uita, take the book. Uita could not read the book himself, and eventually a man called Ripahau explained its contents to him. The same messages of the Gospel of Luke had also made their way into the heart of Ngākuku. Eventually he and Uita meet, and, joined by their common understanding of the same text, Ngākuku forgives Uita. Instead of human revenge, there is forgiveness and reconciliation.

What *then* follows is an extraordinary tale of the power of the *teaching* of the Gospel, as Ripahau , the man who explained Luke's Gospel to Uita, left Uita's pā and returned to Ōtaki. There he came into contact with Katu Te Rauparaha (later known as Tamihana Te Rauparaha) from Kāpiti, the son of the great Ngāti Toa chief Te Rauparaha. Ripahau was again invited to read from the scripture to Katu and his nephew Te Whiwhi. Some years later Katu Tamihana took Tarore's Gospel with him when he travelled to the South Island to revisit his father's traditional enemies, bringing the gospel of peace there for the first time. I heard recently that that little book was buried beneath the church at Rangiātea when it was built by the senior Te Rauparaha. So, for some of us at least, the text has been imbued with a kind of power.

Tarore's death was not God's will. Some of the tellers of the story today attribute an almost magical aspect to Tarore's death, and to her copy of Luke's Gospel, both somehow leading to the subsequent and immediate evangelisation of Māori. Her blood has been referred to as 'the seed of the Gospel' almost ignoring the teaching role Māori ourselves, particularly Ngākuku himself, had in the spread of the Gospel. It is an understandable response: the forgiveness and reconciliation between Ngākuku and Uita was an extraordinary moment. It is not really possible to overstate its impact. But the aftermath of Tarore's death is really a story of Māori agency, Māori teaching and Māori evangelisation. To refer here to Jeremiah, Māori neighbour teaching Māori neighbour in the hope that we will all have direct knowledge and understanding of God.

There is much we can yet learn from this story. I also don't think we should neglect the role of the Holy Spirit and of the human willingness of these men, Ngākuku and Uita, and the other Māori actors, that saw the subsequent spread of the Gospel. In this story, Māori reached out to seek transformation, to receive grace; they were not passively injected with it, they sought it. We took a leap of faith. Ngākuku himself listened and could, in the worst moment of his life, surrender his own fears and doubts to God. Who among us can say the same?

I'd like to end with the final words of the Reverend Brown about this episode, written on 20 October 1836.

> Let those who treat the operations of the Holy Spirit upon the Heart as an idle fable account, on natural principles, for the scene I have this day been privileged to witness. It was not insensibility on the part of Ngākuku, for his feelings are naturally keen. It was not indifference towards his family, for he was firmly attached to his child. No; it was the manifestation of His power, who, amidst the loudest howlings of the wildest storm, distinctly whispers to His Children, it is I. Do not be afraid, peace. Be still.[1]

Mana Wahine, the Legal System and the Search for Better Stories

JUNE 2017

Let me tell you a short story about an old court case. This case is well known to those familiar with New Zealand legal history. It involves a woman called Waipapakura from the Ngāti Hineuru hapū of Te Āti Awa. One day in 1911 she used nets on poles to go fishing in the tidal waters of the Waitōtara River, west of Whanganui. History doesn't tell us if the fish were biting that day, just that she stuck her poles in the riverbed and got to work. At some point, a fisheries officer came along, told her she wasn't allowed to do what she was doing, and took her poles and nets away. Just one small story of Māori having their practices interrupted or obliterated by Those Who Knew Better. On this occasion the woman bit back and sued the officer for the return of her nets. Keep her story in mind. We'll return to it shortly.

The stories that others tell about us can also come to define us; even when they are false, because they often hold pieces of truth that wound, like tiny unseen shards of broken glass.

Our legal system is the source of many stories about Māori in New Zealand society, including the broad and depressing story of how we have become, in the last forty years, a hyper-incarcerated people, arrested, locked up, and more heavily punished for criminal behaviour than our population numbers warrant.

There are other older stories too; of how Māori have been excluded, ignored, discriminated against and plundered by way of the legal system over the course of the past 175 years or so. We need little reminding of these bad and true stories; of the lands stolen, confiscated, and lost, often completely 'legally'; of customary marriages and family relationships being ignored or trampled; of the depletion of our language and cultural practices.

In this powerful story of exclusion and loss, the position of Māori *women* has often been unseen, because the New Zealand legal system has also long failed to recognise women and children anyway. The notion that Māori women could have specific rights, authority, cultural expressions, tikanga, or even opinions that required protection or attention was usually anathema to the New Zealand legal system in the nineteenth and twentieth centuries.

This exclusion of the voices and mana of wāhine Māori began very early. In nineteenth-century Māori society important decisions were often made in hui rūnanga. Māori women were integral to such gatherings, as noted in one of the pro-government Māori newspapers of the time, which bemoaned such mana being afforded women's voices:

> [W]ith the Maori Runanga, all must assemble together, the small and the great, the husband, the wife, the old

> man, the old woman and the children, the knowing and the foolish, the thoughtful and the presumptuous: these all obtain admittance to the Runanga Maori, with all their thoughts and speeches: this woman gets up and has her talk, and that youth gets up and has his …
>
> Who ever arranged it that the (whole) village should turn-out for the settlement of disputes? … And who ever supposed that all the women and children should go and listen to the adulterous cases of bad men? … The Pakeha's plan in such a case is different. When a case of adultery is to be heard, neither women nor young people are allowed to hear the evidence; it is called out that they must all go outside … there are none left sitting in the Court-house on such occasions, but the male adults only. Let the Maories do likewise. Let them, by no means, allow the women and children to hear what is said about such an evil, lest they should understand all, and desire it themselves.[1]

The writer ultimately got his wish, and as the constitution developed over time, including the court system in New Zealand, the mana, needs and rights of Māori women became all but invisible.

Back to Waipapakura and her confiscated fishing nets. Here's what happened. The court said Waipapakura had no right to use her own nets as she did, *even though* she was a customary owner of the land on which the fishing took place. The court found Māori had no right to sink fishing poles into the foreshore and seabed. Only Māori rights specifically affirmed by statute could be recognised in the New Zealand courts. *Her* rights were not affirmed in statute, so were ignored. (*Waipapakura v Hempton* (1914) 33 NZLR 1065 (SC))

Many would say, rightly, that this decision occurred because the legal system has always been institutionally racist, unable and unwilling to recognise Māori customs, values, tikanga and concepts, let alone the lives of Māori women. Would things be different today? There is now precedent for recognising Māori rights over and above the Treaty, and for recognising such rights outside the express terms of legislation.

But much depends on the storyteller. The storytellers *par excellence* in the legal system are judges. Judges hear the stories brought to them in the courtroom, and in judging, construct a narrative that becomes law. The majority of judges writing the stories that flow out of our courtrooms and into our law are still male and Pākehā. Those factors alone don't preclude true justice being given to those affected by their decisions; what does so are the values and beliefs that such judges inevitably bring to the task of judging.

By virtue of the cases handed down to us, we know that New Zealand judges, over the course of our legal history, have rarely held values and beliefs that recognised let alone respected the particular needs and roles of Māori women, or Māori generally, for that matter. But we are not bound to repeat the blindness of the past.

A forthcoming book: *Feminist Judgments of Aotearoa New Zealand: Te Rino, A Two-Stranded Rope* shows how changing our stories can be possible.[2] In an exercise of imagination, participants took twenty-five judgments from New Zealand legal history and rewrote them, as if each judgment author was one of the judges sitting at the time of the original decision. Nineteen of the judgments applied a feminist lens through which to view the exact same material as the original judge. The book also incorporates six judgments rewritten from the perspective of mana wahine; applying thinking and analysis that upholds the mana of Māori women and centralises Māori experiences and Māori world-views in the rewriting of such judgments.

So what happened when the Waipapakura decision was rewritten as a part of the project? Well, the judge (Emma Gattey, in this case) decided that, as an exercise of a customary right, Waipapakura *was* entitled to fish (even if general fishing regulations didn't allow the use of her nets) *especially because* she was a customary owner of the land on which the fishing took place. In making this decision, the court declined to follow numerous doctrines of colonial law, finding them contrary to higher authority or principle. Waipapakura, in this alternative reality, got her nets back, and her story as a provider for her people was allowed to continue.

This rewritten judgment is not mere wish fulfilment. A mana wahine-based reading of the law was possible at that time, even within the strictures of the colonial legal system. *It could have happened.* So along with the other mana wahine judgments, and feminist rewritten judgments ranging between 1914 and 2015, these new (albeit fictional) stories of what could have been give hope that the story of Māori women, and Māori generally, and the legal system, can change; can become different.

Time, as always, will tell her own story.

Note on the Text

Most of these pieces originally appeared on the blog Sparrowhawk/Kārearea between 2015 and 2019; some were later posted there.

A number were also published on the online magazine, e-Tangata, in slightly edited form: 'The Only Māori in the Room' (https://e-tangata.co.nz/reflections/the-only-maori-in-the-room/); 'I Never Saw Any Narrative of Māori Life Until I Was an Adult', (https://e-tangata.co.nz/reflections/mamari-stephens-i-never-saw-any-narrative-of-maori-life-until-i-was-an-adult/); 'The Crown Isn't Just Pākehā. It Is Also Māori', (https://e-tangata.co.nz/comment-and-analysis/the-crown-isnt-just-pakeha-it-is-also-maori/); 'What Some Bloody Awful Cartoons Can Tell Us About Ourselves', (https://e-tangata.co.nz/comment-and-analysis/mamari-stephens-what-some-bloody-awful-cartoons-can-tell-us-about-ourselves/); 'What About a Welfare System That Doesn't Judge Need?', (https://e-tangata.co.nz/comment-and-analysis/mamari-stephens-what-about-a-welfare-system-that-doesnt-judge-need/); 'Bad Laws Sometimes Deserve Breaking', (https://e-tangata.co.nz/comment-and-analysis/bad-laws-sometimes-deserve-breaking/); 'Why Is God and Sexuality so Bloody Difficult?', (https://e-tangata.co.nz/reflections/why-is-god-and-sexuality-so-bloody-difficult/); 'A Good Death', (https://e-tangata.co.nz/comment-and-analysis/a-good-death/?fbclid=IwAR

2SnYieodzr3WsR_4teRZxyEEid8hjHX-q76jryw5P-F0W0eHMGN4okV3Q); 'The Empathy Gap and Me', (https://e-tangata.co.nz/comment-and-analysis/the-empathy-gap-and-me/).

'Reading the Signs on a Journey into Māori Law' was first published in *Ngā Kete Mātauranga: Māori Scholars at the Research Interface*, edited by Jacinta Ruru and Linda Waimarie Nikora, Otago University Press, Dunedin, 2021. It was later published in e-Tangata (https://e-tangata.co.nz/reflections/reading-the-signs-on-a-journey-into-maori-law/).

'The Long Shadow Over Our Marae' was published in *The Journal of Urgent Writing, Volume 2, 2017*, edited by Simon Wilson, Massey University Press, Auckland, 2017. It was later published, with permission, on e-Tangata (https://e-tangata.co.nz/reflections/mamari-stephens-the-long-shadow-over-our-marae/).

'Mana Wahine, the Legal System & the Search for Better Stories' was originally published in the June/July 2017 issue of *Mana Magazine*.

'Teaching and Learning' was an unpublished sermon, given 19 October 2019.

The articles have been selected, arranged and edited for this publication. The date each piece was originally written appears at the start of each chapter. The copyright holders are gratefully acknowledged for their permission to reproduce these pieces.

Notes

The Only Māori in the Room

1 Joanna Kidman, Cherie Chu, Sean Fernandez and Ivy Abella, *Māori Scholars and the University*, Victoria University of Wellington, December 2015.

2 Mihingarangi Forbes, 'Hui Aims To Get More Māori Working in Tech', RNZ, 26 August 2016, rnz.co.nz/news/te-manu-korihi/311854/hui-aims-to-get-more-maori-working-in-tech (accessed August 2016).

Casual Racism and the Phone Message of Doom

1 Martyn Bradbury, 'Marae TV Phone Message Racism Highlights Ignorance', Waatea, 28 May 2017, https://waateanews.com/2017/05/28/marae-tv-phone-message-racism-highlights-ignorance (accessed 17 November 2021).

I Never Saw Any Narrative of Māori Life Until I Was an Adult

1 Project Implicit, implicit.harvard.edu (accessed March 2018).

2 Māoriland, maorilandfilm.co.nz (accessed March 2018).

The Crown Isn't Just Pākehā – It Is Also Māori

1 'Old Government Buildings', Heritage New Zealand Pouhere Taonga, heritage.org.nz/places/places-to-visit/wellington-region/old-government-buildings (accessed October 2017).

2 Tina Law, 'Thousands Queue to See Christchurch's New Justice Precinct', Stuff, 17 September 2017, stuff.co.nz/the-press/news/96927723/thousands-queue-to-see-christchurch-s-new justice-precinct (accessed October 2017).

3 Annabelle Tukia, 'Christchurch's New Justice Precinct Opens For Public', Newshub, 17 September 2017, newshub.co.nz/home/new-zealand/2017/09/Christchurch-s-new-justice-precinct-opens-for-public.html (accessed October 2017).

4 *Tū Mai Te Rangi! Report on the Crown and Disproportionate Offending Rates, Waitangi Tribunal Report*, Waitangi Tribunal, Wellington, 2017, forms.justice.govt.nz/search/Documents/WT/wt_DOC_121273708/Tu%20Mai%20Te%20Rangi%20W.pdf (accessed October 2017).

5 Te Kuru o te Marama Dewes, 'Police Cop Flak For Māori-Designed Police Car', Te Ao Māori News, 13 September 2017, teaomaori.news/police-cop-flak-maori-designed-police-car (accessed October 2017).
6 Te Aniwa Hurihanganui, 'Corrections Launches New Haka to Get More Māori Workers', RNZ, 20 July 2017, rnz.co.nz/news/te-manu-korihi/335510/corrections-launches-new-haka-to-get-more-maori-workers (accessed October 2017).
7 'Q&A Kingi Snelgar: On the Limits & Frustration of a White Legal System', Impolitikal, 4 September 2017, impolitikal.com/2017/09/04/qa-kingi-snelgar-on-the-limits-frustrations-of-a-white-legal-system (accessed October 2017).
8 Māmari Stephens, 'St Bede & the Law Student (and My Grumpy Father)' (blogpost), 31 March 2015, Sparrowhawk/Kārearea, https://sparrowhawkkarearea.com/2015/03/ (accessed October 2017).
9 *Wai 262, Te Reo Māori, Waitangi Tribunal Report*, Waitangi Tribunal, Wellington, 2010, p.51, tetaurawhiri.govt.nz/assets/MLS-documents/1b1d8d6505/Wai-262-PDF.pdf (accessed October 2017).

What Some Bloody Awful Cartoons Can Tell Us About Ourselves

1 'Engineering Students' Haka: Being Confronted', in 'Ngā Rōpū Tautohetohe – Māori Protest Movements', Te Ara – The Encyclopedia of New Zealand, teara.govt.nz/en/photograph/35953/engineering-students-haka-being-confronted (accessed May 2017).
2 Amie Berghan Paulet, 'The Words Sitting at the Tip of My Tongue That I Need to Share', in *Cronecle: Newsletter of the Lower Hutt Women's Centre*, 28, 1 (2020), p.10, https://lhwc.org.nz/wp-content/uploads/2020/12/FinalDecember2020Newsletter.pdf (accessed 15 November 2021).
3 Joelle Dally and Michael Daly, '"Racist" Cartoon Slammed', Stuff, 30 May 2013, stuff.co.nz/ipad-editors-picks/8736295/Racist-cartoon-slammed (accessed May 2017).
4 Michael Wright, 'Tribunal Finds "Provocative" Fairfax Cartoons Did Not Breach Human Rights Act', Stuff, 12 May 2017, stuff.co.nz/national/92502908/tribunal-finds-provocative-fairfax-cartoons-did-not-breach-human-rights-act (accessed May 2017).
5 *Decision of Human Rights Tribunal* [2017] NZHRRT17, p.51, justice.govt.nz/assets/Documents/Decisions/wall-v-fairfax-new-zealand-ltd-2017-nzhrrt-17.pdf (accessed May 2017).

What About a Welfare System That Doesn't Judge Need?

1 'Homeless Man Given Food from Children - Then Immediately Throws It to the Ground', *New Zealand Herald*, 7 March 2017, www.nzherald.co.nz/nz/homeless-man-given-food-from-children-then-immediately-throws-it-to-the-ground/MZSRSUJDOVQQ3X6GSWIYX54GCA (accessed 15 November 2021). Note: the comment section for the article has now been removed.

2 Tom O'Connor, 'Millennials and Boomers Need to Stand Together at the Polls', Stuff, 13 March 2017, www.stuff.co.nz/waikato-times/90372159/tom-oconnor-millennials-and-boomers-need-to-stand-together-at-the-polls (accessed April 2017).

3 Jess Berentson-Shaw, 'The Morgan Foundation's Jess Berentson-Shaw Looks in Detail at the MBIE Child Poverty Report to Separate the Trends and Facts from the Political Claims Made by Others Over Its Data', Interest.co.nz, 18 September 2016, interest.co.nz/opinion/83636/morgan-foundations-jess-berentson-shaw-looks-detail-mbie-child-poverty-report-separate (accessed April 2017).

4 New legislation was eventually passed: the Social Security Act 2018, Residential Care and Disability Support Services Act 2018 and Artificial Limb Service Act 2018.

5 Māmari Stephens, 'Will Tūhoe Provide the Welfare Model?', e-Tangata, 30 July 2016, e-tangata.co.nz/comment-and-analysis/will-tuhoe-provide-the-welfare-model/ (accessed April 2017).

6 'Elderly, Young Families First in Line for Gareth Morgan's "Universal Income" Policy', Stuff, 14 March 2017, stuff.co.nz/national/politics/90414366/elderly-young-families-first-in-line-for-gareth-morgans-universal-income-policy (accessed April 2017).

7 Bernard Hickey, 'Opinion: Gareth Morgan Fleshes Out His "Big Kahuna" Idea for a Comprehensive Capital Tax and an Unconditional Basic Income', Interest.co.nz, 2 August 2011, interest.co.nz/opinion/54671/opinion-gareth-morgan-fleshes-out-his-big-kahuna-idea-comprehensive-capital-tax-and (accessed April 2017). Note: Gareth Morgan is no longer associated with the Opportunities Party.

Bad Laws Sometimes Deserve To Be Broken

1 Isaac Davison, 'Green Party Co-Leader Metiria Turei Admits She Lied To WINZ, As Party Announces Radical Welfare Reforms', *New Zealand Herald*, 16 July 2017, nzherald.co.nz/nz/green-party-co-leader-metiria-turei-admits-she-lied-to-winz-as-party-announces-radical-welfare-reforms (accessed July 2017).

2 See 'Veteran Celebrates Historic Bastion Point Protest', Stuff, 31 January 2009, stuff.co.nz/national/458328/Veteran-celebrates-historic-Maori-protest; 'Māori–Pākehā Conflict' in 'Taranaki Region, Te Ara – The Encyclopedia of New Zealand, teara.govt.nz/en/taranaki-region/page-8 (accessed July 2017).

3 The law mentioned in this piece underwent reform in the passage of the Social Security Act 2018. However, the principles discussed in this piece remain, as does the requirement of sole parents to name the other parent (for example) as at 2021, although reform has been long signalled to remove sanctions for benefit recipients who do not identify the other parent.

Te Puea Marae, Tūhoe and the State of (Māori) Welfare

1 Shannon Haunui-Thompson, '16YO With Cancer and Family Moving to New Home', RNZ, 24 June 2016, rnz.co.nz/news/national/307164/16yo-with-cancer-and-family-moving-to-new-home (accessed June 2016).

2 Eleanor Ainge Roy, 'New Zealand Housing Crisis Forces Hundreds to Live in Tents and Garages', *The Guardian*, 17 May 2016, theguardian.com/world/2016/may/17/new-zealand-housing-crisis-forces-hundreds-to-live-in-garages-tents-and-cars (accessed June 2016).

3 Reina Tuai Harris, *Invisible in the SuperCity: Hidden Homelessness in Auckland*, The Salvation Army Social Policy and Parliamentary Unit, Auckland, November 2015, pp.20–21, salvationarmy.org.nz/sites/default/files/uploads/20151118SPPUInvisible%20in%20SuperCity%20Web%20PDF.pdf (accessed June 2016).

4 Shabnam Dastgheib, 'Auckland Housing Crisis Makes More Children and Families Homeless – Report', Stuff, 18 November 2015, https://www.stuff.co.nz/business/money/74149978/auckland-housing-crisis-makes-more-children-and-families-homeless---report (accessed June 2016).

5 Shannon Haunui-Thompson, 'Marae Opens Its Doors to Those in Need', RNZ, 25 May 2016, https://www.rnz.co.nz/news/te-manu-korihi/304785/marae-opens-its-doors-to-those-in-need (accessed June 2016).

6 Harata Brown, 'Manurewa Marae Step Closer to Opening Doors to Homeless', Te Ao Māori News, 25 June 2016, https://www.rnz.co.nz/news/te-manu-korihi/304785/marae-opens-its-doors-to-those-in-need (accessed June 2016).

7 Shannon Haunui-Thompson, 'Marae Opens Its Doors to Those in Need', RNZ, 25 May 2016, https://www.rnz.co.nz/news/te-manu-korihi/304785/marae-opens-its-doors-to-those-in-need (accessed June 2016).

8 Wiremu Tamihana, *Southern Cross*, 6 August 1858, quoted in Evelyn Stokes, *Wiremu Tamihana – Rangatira*, Huia Publishers, Wellington, 2003, p.165.

9 Ann Parsonson, 'Hērangi, Te Kirihaehae Te Puea', from *The Dictionary of New Zealand Biography* in Te Ara – The Encyclopedia of New Zealand, https://teara.govt.nz/en/biographies/3h17/herangi-te-kirihaehae-te-puea (accessed June 2016).

10 Lindsay Mitchell, 'Maori and Separatism' (blogpost), 15 April 2010, https://lindsaymitchell.blogspot.com/2010/04/maori-and-separatism.html (accessed June 2016); '"Mischief" Over Maori Sovereignty Comments', Stuff, 10 February 2015, https://www.stuff.co.nz/national/politics/65982515/mischief-over-maori-sovereignty-comments (accessed June 2016).

11 Māmari Stephens, 'Walk On By? Māori and the "Compassion Gap"' (blogpost), Sparrowhawk/Kārearea, 25 June 2014, https://sparrowhawkkarearea.com/2014/06/25/walk-on-by-maori-and-the-compassion-gap/ (accessed June 2016).

12 David Moore, Graham Scott, Rebecca Drew, Joanne Smith and Claire Whelan, *Decentralising Welfare – Te Mana Motuhake o Tuhoe: Report to the Ministry of Social Development*, Sapere Research Group, Wellington, 2014, http://srgexpert.com/wp-content/uploads/2017/11/Decentralising-welfare-te-mana-motuhake-o-tuhoe.pdf (accessed June 2016).

13 Ibid., p.31.

14 Ibid., p.33.

The Long Shadow Over Our Marae

1 In 2019 this beautiful and complex place was all but destroyed in a fire, auē, te mamae.

2 Rino Tirikatene, *Hansard*, vol. 712, 30 March 2016, p.10072, www.parliament.nz/en/pb/hansard-debates/rhr/document/51HansS_20160330_00001345/tirikatene-rino-building-earthquake-prone-buildings (accessed 19 November 2021).

3 Talisa Kupenga, 'Labour Party Intern Scheme "Slave Labour" – Marama Fox', Te Ao Maori News, 22 June 2017, www.teaomaori.news/labour-party-intern-scheme-slave-labour-marama-fox (accessed 19 November 2021).

4 In 2020, despite this controversy, the Crown renewed the lease to the current incorporated society. Brad Flahive, 'Awataha Marae: Crown Renews Controversial Lease to Wilson Family', Stuff, 15 July 2020, www.stuff.co.nz/pou-tiaki/122128228/awataha-marae-crown-renews-controversial-lease-to-wilson-family (accessed 15 November 2021).

5 Cumberland City Council, Council Meeting Wednesday 19 February 2020, http://cumberland.infocouncil.biz/Open/2020/02/C_19022020_AGN_2681_AT.htm (accessed 19 November 2021).

6 'Historical Data', Australian Bureau of Statistics, www.abs.gov.au/websitedbs/censushome.nsf/home/historicaldata (accessed 19 November 2021).

7 Paul Hamer, 'Māori in Australia: An Update from the 2011 Australian Census and the 2011 New Zealand General Election', *SSRN*, 28 October 2012, p.3.

8 Mason Durie, 'Pae Matatū: Sustaining the Māori Estate', Te Mata o Te Tau Lecture Series, Massey University, 24 June 2009, www.manu-ao.ac.nz/massey/fms/manu-ao/documents/Pae%20Matatu%20-%20Sustaining%20the%20Maori%20Estate.pdf?DBAAF53CF97AC470650CE5624DB1D48B (accessed 19 November 2021).

9 Mason Durie, *Ngā Tini Whetū: Navigating Māori Future*, Huia Publishers, Wellington, 2011, p.361.

Why Is God and Sexuality so Bloody Difficult?

1 Francis Spufford, *Unapologetic: Why, Despite Everything, Christianity Can Still Make Surprising Emotional Sense*, Faber & Faber, London, 2012, p.62 (ebook edition).

2 Israel Folau, PlayersVoice, https://www.playersvoice.com.au/israel-folau-im-a-sinner-too/ (accessed April 2018).

3 Charlotte Brontë, *Jane Eyre*, Duke Classics, 2012, p.716 (ebook edition, first published 1847).

4 'Anglican Church in New Zealand Opens the Door to Blessing Same-Sex Relationships', Anglican Communion News Service, 9 May 2018, https://www.anglicannews.org/news/2018/05/anglican-church-in-new-zealand-opens-the-door-to-blessing-same-sex-relationships.aspx (accessed May 2018).

5 'Sexuality Working Group Recommends Services of Blessing Without Changing Formularies', Anglican Communion News Service, 22 January 2018, https://www.anglicannews.org/news/2018/01/sexuality-working-group-recommends-services-of-blessing-without-changing-formularies.aspx (accessed April 2018).

6 Charlie Gates, 'Splinter Group Splits from Anglican Church over Same-Sex Blessings', Stuff, 4 September 2018, https://www.stuff.co.nz/national/106783672/splinter-group-splits-from-anglican-church-over-samesex-blessings (accessed April 2018).

7 Paul Peachey, 'African Anglicans May Trigger Formal Schism of Church at Canterbury Meeting', *Independent*, 10 January 2016, https://www.independent.co.uk/news/uk/home-news/

african-anglicans-may-trigger-formal-schism-church-canterbury-meeting-a6805176.html (accessed April 2018).

A Good Death

1 Māmari Stephens, 'Euthanasia: In Defence of the Little Moments of True Life' (blogpost), Sparrowhawk/Kārearea, 9 June 2017, https://sparrowhawkkarearea.com/?s=euthanasia (accessed June 2019).

2 'End of Life Choice Bill', New Zealand Legislation, https://www.legislation.govt.nz/bill/member/2017/0269/latest/whole.html#contents (accessed June 2019).

3 'The Suicide Pact That Shook the World on Euthanasia: Daughter of Pat and Peter Shaw on Why She's Happy They Went on Their Own Terms', *New Zealand Herald*, 26 January 2016, https://www.nzherald.co.nz/nz/the-suicide-pact-that-shook-the-world-on-euthanasia-daughter-of-pat-and-peter-shaw-on-why-shes-happy-they-went-on-their-own-terms/EI3HHDRZIR4LLD (accessed June 2019).

4 Henry Samuel, 'Belgium Authorised Euthanasia of a Terminally Ill Nine and 11-Year-Old in Youngest Cases Worldwide', *The Telegraph*, 7 August 2018, www.telegraph.co.uk/news/2018/08/07/belgium-authorised-euthanasia-terminal-ly-nine-11-year-old-youngest (accessed 19 November 2021).

5 Dame Tariana Turia, 'Euthanasia Would Undermine Whānau Values', *New Zealand Herald*, 1 April 2019, https://www.nzherald.co.nz/kahu/best-of-2019-dame-tariana-turia-euthanasia-would-undermine-whanau-values/3ECF6JZZ2RP5FF3LRN4FDMF32Q/ (accessed June 2019)

6 'End of Life Choice Bill As Reported From the Justice Committee', p.19, https://www.parliament.nz/resource/en-NZ/SCR_86640/c5b7adfc7598b85747ff94855bc46bfb40470db0 (accessed June 2019).

7 Ibid., p.20.

8 Tess Moeke-Maxwell, Linda Waimarie Nikora and Ngahuia Te Awekotuku, 'End-of-Life Care and Māori Whānau Resilience', *MAI Journal*, 3, 2 (2014), p.150, http://www.journal.mai.ac.nz/sites/default/files/MAI_Jrnl_V3_iss2_Maxwell.pdf (accessed June 2019).

9 Judgment of J. Collins, *Seales v Attorney-General* [2015] NZHC 1239 [4 June 2015], p.22 [77], https://forms.justice.govt.nz/search/Documents/pdf/jdo/bb/alfresco/service/api/node/content/workspace/SpacesStore/f7827140-86db-46a4-b8b7-2d8bd8d890d0/f7827140-86db-46a4-b8b7-2d8bd8d890d0.pdf (accessed June 2019).

10 'Euthanasia Bill Could Threaten Vulnerable Māori If It Becomes Law – Advocacy Group', 1News, 10 April 2019, https://www.1news.co.nz/2019/04/10/euthanasia-bill-could-threaten-vulnerable-maori-if-it-becomes-law-advocacy-group/ (accessed June 2019).

11 Laura Walters, 'Disability Rights Commissioner Opposes Assisted Dying Bill', Stuff, 7 March 2019, https://www.stuff.co.nz/national/politics/102046196/disability-rights-commissioner-opposes-assisted-dying-bill (accessed June 2019).

12 'Open Statement on the End of Life Choice Bill', Lawyers for Vulnerable New Zealanders, https://lvnz.org/statement/ (accessed June 2019).

13 'End of Life Choice Bill', New Zealand Legislation, https://www.legislation.govt.nz/bill/member/2017/0269/latest/whole.html#contents (accessed June 2019).

14 Ruby Macandrew and Thomas Manch, 'Significant Changes to End of Life Choice Bill Proposed By David Seymour', Stuff, 14 December 2018, https://www.stuff.co.nz/national/health/euthanasia-debate/109351644/significant-changes-to-end-of-life-choice-bill-proposed-by-david-seymour (accessed June 2019).

15 Jeremy Rees, 'Assisted Dying Divides Anglican Bishops', Newsroom, 4 July 2018, https://www.newsroom.co.nz/2018/07/02/137651/anglican-bishops-oppose-euthanasia-law (accessed June 2019).

The Empathy Gap and Me

1 'Prison Facts and Statistics – June 2018', Department of Corrections Ara Poutama Aotearoa, https://www.corrections.govt.nz/resources/statistics/quarterly_prison_statistics/prison_stats_june_2018#ethnicity (accessed December 2018)

2 *Tū Mai Te Rangi! Report on the Crown and Disproportionate Offending Rates, Waitangi Tribunal Report*, Waitangi Tribunal, Wellington, 2017, p.11, forms.justice.govt.nz/search/Documents/WT/wt_DOC_121273708/Tu%20Mai%20Te%20Rangi%20W.pdf (accessed December 2018).

3 Alison Chetwin, Tony Waldegrave and Kiri Simonsen, *Speaking About Cultural Background at Sentencing: Section 16 of the Criminal Justice Act 1985*, Ministry of Justice, Wellington, November 2000, https://www.justice.govt.nz/assets/Documents/Publications/section-16.pdf (accessed December 2018).

4 Sentencing Act 2002, s 27(1), www.legislation.govt.nz/act/public/2002/0009/59.0/DLM135583.html (accessed 19 November 2021).

5 'More on Mason: Cultural Factors in Sentencing', *Māori Law Review*, February 2013, http://maorilawreview.co.nz/2013/02/more-on-mason-cultural-factors-in-sentencing/ (accessed December 2018).

6 Tariana Turia, 'Trauma and Colonisation' (speech), 9 March 2002, Beehive.govt.nz, https://www.beehive.govt.nz/speech/trauma-and-colonisation (accessed December 2018).

7 Juliet Gerrard, *Every 4 Minutes: A Discussion Paper on Preventing Family Violence in New Zealand*, Office of the Prime Minister's Chief Science Advisor, Auckland, 6 November 2018, https://cpb-ap-se2.wpmucdn.com/blogs.auckland.ac.nz/dist/f/688/files/2020/02/Every-4-minutes-A-discussion-paper-on-preventing-family-violence-in-New-Zealand.-Lambie-report-8.11.18-x43nf4.pdf (accessed December 2018).

8 Sylvia Ashton-Martyn and Laura O'Connell Rapira, *They're Our Whānau: A Community Powered and Collaborative Report on Māori Perspectives of New Zealand's Justice System*, ActionStation, Wellington, 2018.

9 'Bail Law Changes Led to Prison Population Increase – Little', RNZ, 24 February 2018, https://www.rnz.co.nz/news/political/351162/bail-law-changes-led-to-prison-population-increase-little (accessed December 2018).

Teaching and Learning

1 'Report from the Select Committee of the House of Lords Appointed to Inquire into the Present State of the Lands of New Zealand', 1838, p.203, https://play.google.com/store/books/details?id=BTlDAAAAcAAJ&rdid=book-BTlDAAAAcAA-J&rdot=1 (accessed 19 November 2021).

Mana Wahine, the Legal System and the Search for Better Stories

1 *Te Manuhiri Tuarangi and Maori Intelligencer*, 1 August 1861, p.10.

2 Elisabeth McDonald, Rhonda Powell, Māmari Stephens and Rosemary Hunter (eds), *Feminist Judgments of Aotearoa New Zealand: Te Rino, A Two-Stranded Rope*, Hart Publishing, Portland, Oregon, 2017.

Acknowledgements

Writing is the result of a kind of alchemy I don't really understand. Many of us struggle to arrange our words in ways that make sense, let alone in ways that are pleasing or useful, or both, to a reader. I am grateful for the gift I have been given, aware that many may not find it for themselves. Thank you so much to Bridget Williams, Tom Rennie, Anna Hodge, Nancy Swarbrick, Laura Koziol, and the rest of the BWB team that seemed to want this book to happen. Thank you for your patience with me.

I am also grateful to Gary Wilson and Tapu Misa, who have coaxed so many Māori and Pacific writers out into the light and given them a platform by way of e-Tangata. They both understand the value of the personal voice saying things that matter to the rest of us. Gary also taught me not to be a tosser with flash words. Hei whakakapi, nei rā te mihi aroha ki a koutou, kaituhi mā, o tēnei ao hurihuri, ki tōku whānau anō hoki.

About the Author

Māmari Stephens (Te Rarawa) is an Ahunuku/Reader in Law at Te Kauhanganui Tātai Ture/Faculty of Law, Te Herenga Waka Victoria University of Wellington. A significant contributor to Te Kaupapa Reo-a-Ture/The Legal Māori Project, she recently completed the first comprehensive textbook on social security law. Māmari is a Kaimanaaki, pirihi/Māori chaplain and Anglican priest, and has been a regular writer for e-Tangata and her own blog: Sparrowhawk/Kārearea (www.sparrowhawkkarearea.com).

About BWB Texts

BWB Texts are short books on big subjects from great New Zealand writers. They are succinct narratives spanning contemporary issues, memoir, history and science. With well over fifty BWB Texts in print and more available digitally, new works are published regularly. BWB Texts can be purchased from all good bookstores and online from www.bwb.co.nz.

BWB Texts include:

Kāinga: People, Land, Belonging
Paul Tapsell

He Pou Hiringa: Grounding Science and Technology in Te Ao Māori
Maria Amoamo, Merata Kawharu and Katharina Ruckstuhl (eds)

The History of a Riot
Jared Davidson

100% Pure Future: New Zealand Tourism Renewed
Sarah Bennett (ed.)

Two Hundred and Fifty Ways to Start an Essay about Captain Cook
Alice Te Punga Somerville

Living with the Climate Crisis: Voices from Aotearoa
Tom Doig (ed.)

The Platform: The Radical Legacy of the Polynesian Panthers
Melani Anae

Shouting Zeros and Ones: Digital Technology, Ethics and Policy in New Zealand
Andrew Chen (ed.)

Beyond These Shores: Aotearoa and the World
Nina Hall (ed.)

Imagining Decolonisation
Various

The Climate Dispossessed: Justice for the Pacific in Aotearoa?
Teall Crossen

Transforming the Welfare State: Towards a New Social Contract
Jonathan Boston

#NoFly
Shaun Hendy

Rebuilding the Kāinga: Lessons from Te Ao Hurihuri
Jade Kake

The Broken Estate: Journalism and Democracy in a Post-Truth World
Mel Bunce

Student Political Action in New Zealand
Sylvia Nissen

A Careful Revolution: Towards a Low-Emissions Future
David Hall (ed.)

The Health of the People
David Skegg

Still Counting
Marilyn Waring

Maui Street
Morgan Godfery

Mountains to Sea
Mike Joy (ed.)

Ko Taranaki Te Maunga
Rachel Buchanan

False Divides
Lana Lopesi

A Matter of Fact: Talking Truth in a Post-Truth World
Jess Berentson-Shaw

Better Lives: Migration, Wellbeing and New Zealand
Julie Fry and Peter Wilson

Doing Our Bit: The Campaign to Double the Refugee Quota
Murdoch Stephens

Thought for Food: Why What We Eat Matters
John D. Potter

Island Time: New Zealand's Pacific Futures
Damon Salesa

Portacom City: Reporting on the Christchurch and Kaikōura Earthquakes
Paul Gorman

The Ground Between: Navigating the Oil and Mining Debate in New Zealand
Sefton Darby

Sea Change: Climate Politics and New Zealand
Bronwyn Hayward

The Best of e-Tangata
Edited by Tapu Misa and Gary Wilson

Antibiotic Resistance: The End of Modern Medicine?
Siouxsie Wiles

Hopes Dashed?: The Economics of Gender Inequality
Prue Hyman

Safeguarding the Future: Governing in an Uncertain World
Jonathan Boston

The Stolen Island: Searching for 'Ata
Scott Hamilton

First published in 2021 by Bridget Williams Books Ltd
PO Box 12474, Wellington 6144, New Zealand
www.bwb.co.nz, info@bwb.co.nz.

ISBN 9781990046292 (Paperback), ISBN 9781990046261 (EPUB),
ISBN 9781990046278 (Kindle), ISBN 9781990046285 (PDF)
DOI https://doi.org/10.7810/9781990046292

A catalogue record for this book is available from the National Library of New Zealand. Kei te pātengi raraunga o Te Puna Mātauranga o Aotearoa te whakarārangi o tēnei pukapuka.

The publisher warmly acknowledges the significance of the ongoing support provided by the Bridget Williams Books Publishing Trust. The generous contribution from Ockham Residential for the BWB Texts series is gratefully acknowledged. The commitment of Creative New Zealand to good New Zealand publishing is also acknowledged, and its support for this publication is appreciated.

OCKHAM RESIDENTIAL

creative nz
ARTS COUNCIL OF NEW ZEALAND TOI AOTEAROA

Publisher: Tom Rennie
Editors: Anna Hodge and Nancy Swarbrick
Cover design: Neil Pardington Design
Internal design and typesetting: Katrina Duncan
Printer: Blue Star, Wellington